17·99 ✓

 **NatWe**st   D0357903

BUSINESS HANDBOOKS

If you are running your own business then you probably do not have time for the general, theoretical and often impenetrable subject areas covered by many business and management books. What works for the major corporation may not work for you. What you do need is to-the-point guidance on how to implement sound business skills in a growing enterprise.

The NatWest Business Handbooks deliver this practical advice in an easy-to-follow format.

Written by authors with many years' experience and who are still actively involved in the day-to-day running of successful businesses, these handbooks provide all the guidance you need to tackle the everyday issues that you and your business face. They will enable you to adopt a step-by-step approach to isolating and resolving problems and help you meet the entrepreneurial and organisational challenges of a growing business.

♻ NatWest

BUSINESS HANDBOOKS

A BUSINESS PLAN

Build a great plan for the growing business

Third Edition

ALAN WEST

FINANCIAL TIMES MANAGEMENT
128 Long Acre, London WC2E 9AN
Tel: +44 (0)171 447 2000
Fax: +44 (0)171 240 5771
Website: www.ftmanagement.com

An imprint of Pearson Education Limited

First published in Great Britain in 1987
This edition published in Great Britain in 1998

© Financial Times Professional Limited 1998

ISBN 0 273 63562 X

British Library Cataloguing in Publication Data
A CIP catalogue record for this book can be obtained from the British Library.

Transferred to digital printing 2004

Typeset by Northern Phototypesetting Co. Ltd, Bolton
Printed and bound by Antony Rowe Ltd, Eastbourne

The Publishers' policy is to use paper manufactured from sustainable forests.

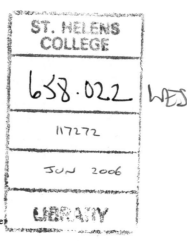

About the Author

Alan West worked as a line manager for Unilever, Mars and Grand Metropolitan, in Europe, the Middle and Far East. He has broad experience of both consulting and training the small and medium enterprise sector.

Alan's knowledge of the practicalities of the creation and management of the business plan has developed from writing large numbers of business plans for a wide variety of companies in the industrial, consumer and service sectors, and working with such enterprises over the last 15 years.

A Business Plan has been translated into seven languages and is one of the 12 business and management texts written by the author.

Alan West can be contacted at 100023.3247@compuserve.com

Research on business planning is collated at the Business Plan website www.tangleweb.co.uk/ibis

Contents

Contents

Why plan?

Introduction • The average SME

Why the business plan is so important to the SME

Business planning and financial performance

What the SME wants from a business plan

Creating control and planning loops

Who can use this book • How to use this book

What you will get from this book

And finally, some general points • Summary

INTRODUCTION

To the entrepreneur, the small- to medium-sized enterprise (SME) has a beauty of its own – security, adaptability, profitability, to name a few. These may indeed be found in those SMEs that are both successful and well run. Yet, it is also true that these are not characteristics of the average SME, which needs planning – and the effective implementation of plans – to ensure that scarce resources are focused in areas that matter. That is what this book is all about.

THE AVERAGE SME

The familiar picture of the average SME is of a business that muddles along from day to day. It is not in control – that is the privilege of outside circumstances. Its executives see little point to planning as a feature of management and there is a general failure to appreciate that using it to look forward, even a little, can be a very effective method

> *The average SME ... needs planning – and the effective implementation of plans – to ensure that scarce resources are focused in areas that matter.*

of both easing current difficulties and anticipating possible problem areas.

Because they are wary of planning – seeing it as something that is too complicated and resource-intensive – managers often fail to see that the nature of their normal day-to-day muddling may well alter the longer their company survives. Yet, to outsiders, like myself, the common problems of SMEs can, and do, vary over time as follows:

- getting established in the first one or two years – finding and keeping customers, developing products or services;
- consolidation in the next period – finding and keeping competent staff, delegating, controlling the business;
- problems of expansion in the next phase – attracting investors, competing with much bigger firms in their markets.

However, SMEs' resources are under severe pressure in a variety of ways:

- they have few employees and managers, skills are limited and expertise scarce;
- money is always a problem, but their managers also have few skills to make the best use of what there is;
- a small management team – usually the partners in the business with highly specialised skills – which is often also learning the main problems of the business as it goes and therefore always experiences time pressures;
- a fairly narrowly defined geographic and industry sector;
- premises that are not totally suitable for the particular business;
- inappropriate use of information for decision making by management – managers relying on historic information, which is often based on externally prepared annual accounts that may be at least one year out of date.

WHY THE BUSINESS PLAN IS SO IMPORTANT TO THE SME

Successful business is about the efficient allocation of scarce resources. Large, well-established companies with loads of money can be, and often are, wasteful, but this is hidden from view because they go broke less often than the SME. With fewer resources, the SME has to be more effective to survive than the large company. It may, arguably, have a greater need for planning as this is central to efficient resource allocation in a variety of ways.

Successful business is about the efficient allocation of scarce resources. Large, well-established companies with loads of money can be, and often are, wasteful ... With fewer resources, the SME has to be more effective to survive.

- Planning identifies areas of the business that are not completely under control but which need urgent action before a realistic approach can be made to outside investors.
- Planning is an important source of information about a company's prospects for funding organisations, such as banks or local

government. Large organisations are generally more successful in gaining access to finance and this is often because they are able to provide more detailed justifications for their requirements.

American research on SMEs suggests that the stability of growth measured over a period of five to ten years is closely correlated to the amount of planning that the company has carried out.

- Planning provides a framework for informing employees and others about the company's future direction.
- Planning helps ensure that management decisions are based on objective analysis of the company's strengths and weaknesses. It also makes management aware of whether they are maximising the financial return on their use of scarce resources and ensures that the team considers the future strategy of the firm.
- Planning demands that management information systems be improved, which benefits all other decision making within the organisation.
- Planning identifies key areas where the firm needs to develop expertise.
- Planning provides a basis for analysing whether or not a new product or process will be a success. It also makes managers more expert about competition in the marketplace.

The average SME can be regarded as viable if it merely survives the first five years of its existence. Research shows that approximately 85 per cent of businesses fail in the first five years, with problems being most acute in the building, light engineering and fashion industries.

However, American research on SMEs suggests that the stability of growth measured over a period of five to ten years is closely correlated to the amount of planning that the company has carried out. While short-term success does not appear to be greatly affected by the amount of planning done, good planning is fundamental to long-term, profitable survival. Dutch research suggests that every day an SME spends planning, it increases its chance of survival by 3 per cent – up to a plateau of 14 days, beyond which no further improvement occurs.

Professionally produced business plans also significantly

improve the prospects of the SME receiving external funding. Research on venture capital funding suggests that a fully detailed plan is 15 times more likely to receive funding than one that is not. Also, bank research suggests that well-prepared business plans receive, on average, double the amount of support of poorly prepared plans. Finally, approval for grants and loans also depends on well-prepared supporting documentation.

BUSINESS PLANNING AND FINANCIAL PERFORMANCE

Throughout the 1980s, SMEs as a group were more profitable than large companies. During the 1990s, the position reversed, with large companies being consistently more profitable than SMEs. Commentators consider that this trend will continue as large companies learn and apply the advantages of SMEs – improved customer service, faster decision making, greater staff motivation in small units – yet retain their existing advantages of lower cost base, market knowledge, staff skills and higher rates of new product or service development.

This process can be taken to be another of the benefits of planning detail: large companies plan, on the whole. By means of planning, they have learned that, in certain areas, the SME has a competitive edge and have set out to correct that situation. It is now perhaps time for the SME to return the compliment by establishing detailed planning information systems that will analyse the large company's competitive activities, adapting these to their needs. By focusing activities and controlling resources via planning, the SME will be able to react to this changing competitive relationship, building large company advantages onto a small company base.

⇨ **Just because your company is small and wants to remain so, does not mean that you cannot improve on large company performance.**

WHAT THE SME WANTS FROM A BUSINESS PLAN

To become a useful business development tool, any plan must take account of the peculiar operational circumstances of the SME. It should meet three criteria:

- simplicity;
- accuracy;
- usefulness.

The exact detail of the plan will vary by company and year. Some business plans are for internal use; others need to be prepared for external funding or for external shareholders' approval. A fully comprehensive list would include all the information given in Table 1.1.

CREATING CONTROL AND PLANNING LOOPS

Regardless of what external use a plan is put to, it is fundamentally useless if it is not continually used by the company to achieve implementation. That is, making sure that plans are not just talked about, but acted on, is crucial to their success.

⇨ **Implementation and continued control are critical parts of planning.**

The main purpose of the business plan is to make planning integral to the organisation so that it becomes a continuous monitoring and control process. The business creates a series of targets in the initial plan that will then be used to monitor, review and re-evaluate as the plan develops. It is a process of continual monitoring and checking to ensure that what is planned is actually taking place – the control loop.

Table 1.1 Outline SME business plan

Details	Description	Further information
Management overview	● Contents ● Key points of the plan	
The business and management	● When the business was established, results to date, borrowing history, existing commitments, current accountants, bankers, lawyers	*Chapter 2*
	● Key personnel, their experience, knowledge of the industry, age, education and training	*Chapter 2; Chapter 3; Chapter 4; Chapter 9*
	● Shareholding structure, involvement of major shareholders in other ventures	
	● Number of employees, including working directors, by category	
	● Expected number of employees after 12 months, by category	
	● Reporting structure, internal organisation	*Chapter 4; Chapter 5*
	● Skills level by department	
	● Profitsharing or bonus schemes	
Past history	● Summary of last three years' trading experience	*Chapter 2; Chapter 5*
	● Successes, failures and lessons learnt	
Product or service	● Current product range	*Chapter 2*
	● Current customers	*Chapter 5*
	● Existing customer contracts	*Chapter 4*
	● Status of product development – including percentage of new products in current sales, quality control	*Chapter 2* *Chapter 3* *Chapter 4* *Chapter 5* *Chapter 6* *Chapter 9*
	● Any patent, trademark or copyright protection	*Chapter 5*
Market and competition	● Market size and growth over five years	*Chapter 5*
	● Major competitors	*Chapter 5*
	● Product/service trends	*Chapter 3* *Chapter 5* *Chapter 7*
	● Distribution outlets/service supply points	*Chapter 3* *Chapter 4* *Chapter 5* *Chapter 6*
	● Sales forecasts	*Chapter 3* *Chapter 4*

▶

Table 1.1 continued

Details	Description	Further information
		Chapter 5 *Chapter 6* *Chapter 7* *Chapter 8*
	● Promotional and pricing plan	*Chapter 4* *Chapter 5*
	● Current and future competitive advantage – including any relevant market research	*Chapter 5*
Objectives and strategy	● Business goals – general	*Chapter 2* *Chapter 3* *Chapter 4* *Chapter 5* *Chapter 6* *Chapter 7* *Chapter 8*
	● SWOT (strengths, weaknesses, opportunities, threats) analysis	*Chapter 2* *Chapter 5*
	● Short- and medium-term objectives – specific targets of gross profit, return on capital, new product development, personnel targets	*Chapter 2* *Chapter 3* *Chapter 4* *Chapter 5* *Chapter 6* *Chapter 7* *Chapter 8*
Information system and frequency of reporting	● Accounting methods – cash flow, profit and loss, balance sheet, financial ratios	*Chapter 2* *Chapter 3* *Chapter 4* *Chapter 5* *Chapter 6* *Chapter 7* *Chapter 8*
	● Production efficiencies	*Chapter 3*
	● Marketing efficiencies	*Chapter 3*
	● Personnel efficiencies	*Chapter 3*
	● New product development efficiencies	*Chapter 3*
	● Equipment, layout	*Chapter 3* *Chapter 4* *Chapter 7*
Production/ service supply system	● Product certification	*Chapter 4* *Chapter 5*
	● Supplier agreements	*Chapter 4*
	● Warehousing, physical distribution, order processing	*Chapter 4* *Chapter 5* *Chapter 7*

Details	Description	Further information
Financial performance	● Projections stating assumptions of future performance for at least one year	*Chapter 7*

	● Estimated turnover to include:
	  – balance sheets and profit and loss accounts
	  – monthly cash flow projections
	  – capital expenditure budgets
	  – sensitivity analysis to show effect of 20 per cent increase in sales and 30 per cent decrease
		Chapter 3
		Chapter 5
		Chapter 8

Assumptions	● Main assumptions underlying the plan	*Chapter 8*
Risk assessment and contingency planning	● What the major risk issues are and how the company is planning to overcome them	*Chapter 8*
Action plan	● Responsibilities	*Chapter 7* *Chapter 8*
	● Timescale and key tasks by month – tasks, milestones, success criteria	*Chapter 3* *Chapter 4* *Chapter 5* *Chapter 6* *Chapter 8*
	● Project plan for major investments, including critical path	
Finance required	● Purpose	
	● Level of return on the investment (for large-scale investments, a net present value calculation or some other discounted cash flow)	
	● Total funding required based on projections	
	● Repayment assumptions	
Security available	● Assets available	
	● Assets used as security elsewhere	

The business also – as a separate, but integrated activity – uses this information to improve performance, define new opportunities, choose new directions and create new targets – the planning loop. These two circular processes are being continually integrated via the information system and management decisions, creating two planning loops, which can be shown as a 'doughnut' or 'torus' (see Figure 1.1).

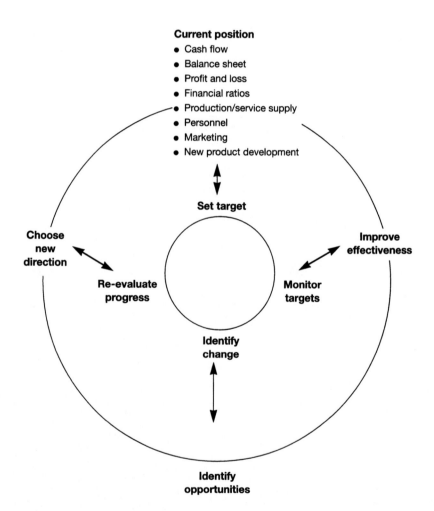

Current position
- Cash flow
- Balance sheet
- Profit and loss
- Financial ratios
- Production/service supply
- Personnel
- Marketing
- New product development

Set target

Choose new direction

Improve effectiveness

Re-evaluate progress

Monitor targets

Identify change

Identify opportunities

Fig. 1.1   The planning cycle

WHO CAN USE THIS BOOK

This book is designed for the SME manager in the service or manufacturing sector. It includes all the practical aspects of creating a business plan and making it work. Because the emphasis is practical, it is also a valuable introduction to the realities of the SME environment for students and individuals considering a career in an SME. In addition, it can help those moving from a functional role in a business into more general management, as the business plan provides an overview of the entire company and how each department interrelates.

Other readers who will find this book useful are those who advise SMEs. Chapter 9 outlines the *business plan health check* (clearly demonstrating another use of planning information and was developed by myself), which is included for them.

A Business Plan is not specifically designed with the problems of the non-profit sector in mind. Many of the issues that are discussed in the book will have relevance to the non-profit sector, but, as I am sure you are aware, the focus of the book is on the creation of clear objectives that are actionable and measurable.

HOW TO USE THIS BOOK

Each chapter develops the business plan in a structured and logical sequence, providing templates for the completion of the plan. Case study material is integrated into the discussion in an attempt to introduce a real-life and practical atmosphere into the development of the business plan. Use your own company as a case study, too, as this will enable you to look at your business objectively and create a realistic business plan.

You will find that the book has been structured around the planning loop in Figure 1.1. You will see that a series of core areas appears under the 'Current position' heading. The book has been written around these core areas, which form a recurring theme throughout the text. They are analysed from different perspectives in each chapter: current company position; building an information system; short-term, corrective action; strategic drivers in the medium and long term; developing strategy, implementing and monitoring the new plan. Table 1.1 also gives some idea of how this works in practice because it includes cross-references to where aspects are discussed in the text.

WHAT YOU WILL GET FROM THIS BOOK

This book provides you with:

- a practical and detailed approach to the development of the business plan – highlighting the key issues for success and failure at each stage;
- case study-based supporting material that provides worked examples of how one manufacturing and one service company develop their plan;
- a format for presenting the plan to outside investors or supporting institutions;
- a management information system that will allow your company to manage the plan as it evolves and control the future of the business.

AND FINALLY, SOME GENERAL POINTS

- Involving as many people as possible in the development of the plan improves the quality of the planning. It also commits a larger number of staff to successful implementation because they have put their ideas into the project.
- Try to do your planning away from the inevitable continual interruptions that occur in the office as thought and concentration are nearly impossible to achieve in such an environment.
- Be brutally realistic about the implementation of the plan. It is easy to create plans on paper – it is when they have to be implemented that they fall apart. It is far better to slightly overachieve a modest target than dramatically underachieve a far more ambitious goal.
- Allocate responsibilities immediately the plan is completed and track action from the earliest days.

- Learn from mistakes – and try not to repeat them.
- A business plan is not designed solely to generate investment cash for the business – it is a skeleton around which the people in the business can think, generate ideas and work so that targets are met and long-term profits are assured.
- A business plan is not a guarantee of success, but it will diminish the chances of failure.

SUMMARY

This chapter has looked at the potential and pitfalls that surround the SME. It summarises the advantages of having a business plan, and lists what a business plan should ideally include – whether it is used to secure external funding or for internal purposes.

Above all, this chapter has stressed the importance of using the business plan to:

- continually measure performance and achievements;
- correct mistakes and move forward;
- attempt to control, rather than react to, events.

Some basic issues

INTRODUCTION

This chapter looks at the important first steps that ought to be clarified as early as possible in the development of the business plan. These include setting general objectives, and an approach to doing this, thereby developing an understanding of what key individuals want from the business and helping to set the key assumptions on which the plan will be based. Because time and action are closely interconnected in this, the planning horizon and the necessity of matching time and action efficiently in the plan are discussed, together with guidance on how to do this. Many of these issues will remain relevant throughout the text.

Another aspect of basic issues needing early clarification in planning is the key quantifiable and specific objectives that the business must consider. One approach to doing this is given here, together with the concept of success and failure analysis to identify major strengths and weaknesses within the organisation and its approach to its market.

This chapter also looks at two company case studies to demonstrate how the concepts work.

THE SURE MNEMONIC

SURE is a mnemonic for specific questions that are at the forefront of planners' minds throughout the book:

- **S** Is the plan *soundly* based? Is it likely to meet a long-term demand in the market?
- **U** Does the business *understand* the relationship between the external market and internal resources – can the plan be implemented?
- **R** Is the plan *realistic*? Plans tend to be optimistic, but does this one overstep reality when compared with previous years' experience?
- **E** Are the previous *experience and expectations* of the group in line with the requirements of the plan?

GENERAL OBJECTIVES – IDENTIFYING COMMON GOALS

To make a plan that is SURE means understanding the general objectives of all those involved in making decisions about the allocation of resources. The business owners, stakeholders (never forget that the bank is a stakeholder) and employees all have expectations or objectives that come from the existing business and how it has developed.

It is vital to understand individuals' expectations, identify where major conflict may exist and, by compromising and discussing, create common goals. Unless such common goals are established, the potential for the plan to be acted on is negligible.

It is vital to understand individuals' expectations, identify where major conflict may exist and, by compromise and discussion, create common goals. Unless such common goals are established, the potential for the plan to be acted on is negligible.

It is sensible to start with general issues and then move on to more specific and quantifiable ones via a series of questions. Help in arriving at realistic and objective answers to these questions can be obtained by looking back at the previous year and considering where the business succeeded and where it failed.

■ General objective 1: Do we want to grow?

The picture often presented of the SME is that of an organisation desperate for growth. The reality is that few SMEs become high-growth operations – in the region of just 1 per cent.

The majority of SMEs have low growth expectations, and the impact this has on the business plan is that of conservatism, directing the business towards maintaining its existing strengths and concentrating on eliminating weaknesses.

A stable business is not necessarily unprofitable or unfulfilling. What is important is whether or not the current and prospective achievements of the business meet the requirements of its key members.

■ General objective 2: Do we want to build a long-term business or is our perspective short-term?

Each decision maker in an SME will have their own target regarding the length of time they want to be involved in creating and developing the business. Different attitudes towards timescales will significantly affect approaches to the plan.

A short-term business horizon tends to concentrate and focus the business into a narrow range of operations and activities to enhance immediate returns. On the other hand, a long-term perspective emphasises the need to reduce short-term expectations in order to create a more broadly based business, enhancing long-term rewards.

■ General objective 3: Do we want to deal with new challenges?

Some businesses have attitudes that favour searches for new challenges, problems and opportunities, while others prefer to remain within established routines and procedures.

How acceptable change is to the decision makers is a fundamental issue. Where they are unhappy or insecure about their ability to deal effectively with change, the company must plan conservatively and build slowly on existing strengths and weaknesses. If they thrive on change, it must be actively sought.

If planning decisions require change, it is important to understand that with new problems comes the need for new solutions. Staff, too, must thrive on getting new things done. Where they are not motivated by the achievement of new and demanding roles, it will be better to remain with existing policies, if they are working.

■ General objective 4: Do we want to maintain control?

Control over the future is one of the main reasons people are attracted to SMEs. Significant changes in direction or in the speed of change will often mean loss of control because more outsiders become involved in the business.

Often an SME fails to develop because the original founder is not prepared to delegate. Effective delegation becomes essential as the business grows, with line managers or supervisors being given the responsibility and authority necessary to carry out specific actions.

This process of delegation is inevitably accompanied by change. Any business that cannot live with significant change must plan with the utmost conservatism. If changes, such as alterations in working practices, hours worked or type of work, are resisted, any ambitious plan will collapse.

■ General objective 5: Do we need a lot of money?

Each shareholder and decision maker within a business will have expectations regarding income over the year. Planning requires that these are clearly and honestly admitted.

■ General objective 6: Will we risk all?

All businesses involve a level of risk, from the minor to the all-consuming. However, when comparing failure rates for large and small companies and the availability of resources, it is probably true that life is riskier for the SME than for larger companies. It is important to understand that all the general objectives discussed so far involve a level of risk. The acceptance of risk – and the potential for failure – must be carefully assessed.

Aggressive plans mean a higher level of risk. Conservative planning can reduce it. Business owners, shareholders, stakeholders and employees must all be happy with the proposed level of risk in the future direction of the business.

CHECKLISTS AND ACTION POINTS

Throughout the book, the emphasis is on building up an understanding of the business with the use of checklists and charts. The first of these helps the business and business planners clarify their general objectives (see Table 2.1).

Table 2.1 Checklist of general objectives

Objective	Completely agree	Largely agree	Agree but with little enthusiasm	Disagree	Violently disagree
1. Do we want to grow?					
2. Perspective long or short term?					
3. Do we want new challenges?					
4. Do we want to maintain control?					
5. High earnings vital?					
6. Risk all?					

THE PLANNING HORIZON

The business plan outlines the necessary action that must be taken immediately, as well as issues that must be considered in the medium and long term. For each business, the planning timescale is a major initial decision. The longer the planning horizon, the more complicated and demanding the analysis.

Because long-term planning makes enormous demands on time and money, it makes sense for the SME to only plan for the length of time that is specifically necessary for its business.

A realistic approach to defining this planning horizon is to consider a combination of how long it takes to develop a new product, and the payback period for that investment. This results in short-term horizons for companies with rapid product development and short paybacks, and long ones for companies with long product development and paybacks. Suggested planning horizons for various types of companies are as follows:

- consultants, fashion, footwear, software: 2 years;
- retail, food, leisure, light engineering: 3 years;
- heavy engineering: 4–5 years.

Within each planning horizon, companies can establish short-, medium- and long-term goals and major implementation issues. The short-term goals should be detailed and fully quantified, the medium- and long-term ones outlined. As the plan develops, the company can and should update the forecast, and continue to create new projections.

⇨ **Only plan over a timescale that relates to the business' requirements.**

QUANTIFIABLE SPECIFIC OBJECTIVES

SMEs can choose from a wide range of quantifiable specific objectives. Experience and research suggest that a limited set of key or specific goals provides the best way of controlling and directing the business. These key objectives also provide a core of information every executive or business planner must be aware of.

Understanding what the business is currently achieving in these specific areas also sets boundaries for future development. For example, it is unrealistic to expect gross margins to improve from 10 to 40 per cent; or for a company historically producing just one new product a year to suddenly produce five or more.

Experience and research suggest that a limited set of key or specific goals provides the best way of controlling and directing the business. These key objectives also provide a core of information every executive or business planner must be aware of.

■ Specific objective 1: Are we improving gross profit levels wherever possible?

What is the current level of gross profit the business achieves? Gross profit is normally defined as the net sales price minus direct costs of materials and labour. It is important because there is a direct relationship between the level of gross profit and the survival potential of the business. One technique for calculating the gross profit ratio is given in Chapter 3.

Those businesses with high gross profit margins survive longer than those without Figure 2.1). The reason is simple – with high margins, the company has an increased ability to make mistakes and survive. Errors on low margins may be fatal.

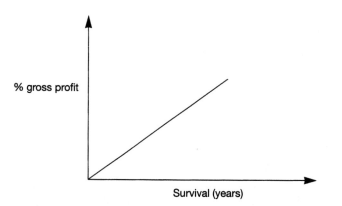

Fig. 2.1   The relationship between gross profit margins and survival

⟹ **Look to increase gross profit margins wherever possible.**

■ Specific objective 2: Are we controlling fixed costs?

What is the current level of fixed costs? Fixed costs are those incurred whether the company is producing goods or services or not – rent, rates, insurance, salaries are all examples. They are vital because they determine the value of goods or services that must be sold to achieve a profit (Figure 2.2).

The equation is a simple one. The total fixed costs of the business are divided by the average gross profit per unit. For example, if:

Fixed costs = £10,000
Margin per unit = £2
Breakeven = 5,000 units

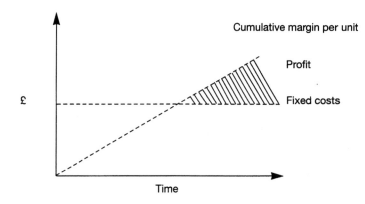

Fig. 2.2   Breakeven assessment

Every business should attempt to reduce its level of fixed costs, so breakeven can be achieved at lower volumes (though, obviously, gross profit also influences breakeven – the higher the gross profit, the lower the breakeven volumes).

➩   **Attack fixed costs wherever possible within the organisation.**

■ Specific objective 3: Are we in control of new product/service development?

What percentage of the profit for last year was provided by new products or services? In a competitive environment, businesses must introduce new products or services far more frequently than where there is little competition, though the speed of change will vary by industry.

A new product or service is defined as one that is perceived by customers as being new and this distinction must be kept in mind. It may be only marginally different from the old to the supplier, but has enormous additional advantages for customers. Experience and research show that, whatever the sector, those companies that are continually refining and altering their products' or services' benefits are generally the most profitable and successful (Figure 2.3). You only have to think of companies of the likes of:

- Siemens
- Ericsson
- Kelloggs
- Compaq

- Nokia
- Glaxo
- 3M
- Hewlett-Packard

- Merck
- Electrolux
- Microsoft.

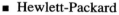

Leaders

Followers

Percentages of turnover by year of introduction are shown in bold.

Fig. 2.3   Leaders and followers

The complication is that new products and services need careful management. Companies starting to develop new products and services without also considering the implications (timescales, costs, manpower, skills) often face enormous problems. Techniques for monitoring new product development are given in Chapter 3 in the discussion of new product development efficiencies.

▷ **Change can provide major competitive advantage, provided that the change is managed.**

■ Specific objective 4: Are we maximising the advantages gained from improvements in the company skills profile?

Do you know whether the skills profile within the company is increasing or decreasing? Such a question is not purely about existing skills – do the personnel have the training and knowledge to deal with new technologies and processes?

In many industries and services, the pace of technology is so fast that a skills level of 100 (expert in all the existing technologies – see below) will become 80 or 70 in the following year. SMEs cannot therefore afford to be static in their approach to skills development, even if they recruit the most skilled and professional staff available at the time.

Keeping staff abreast of changing techniques and technologies is not the only advantage of having a higher skills base. A skilled workforce enables a company to produce higher-quality goods and services, deal with a wider range of problems and be more flexible in its approach to the type of work required. It also requires less supervision, making significant savings on management staff and time.

Training the workforce is also the only sure way of changing the company culture. All organisations start with a clearly defined culture that decides how the business will develop – a culture that is often practically impossible to shift, whatever the demands of the business plan. Training tends to make this sort of culture more flexible by creating new perspectives and new working practices.

A convenient classification is to divide staff into five categories in ascending order of skill:

- **novice** lacks any clear understanding of the overall task and can only judge their performance of the job by reference to published targets;
- **advanced beginner** begins to be able to identify solutions to problems from previous experience, but still lacks an overview of the total task;

- **competent** can set performance targets and expectations from previous experience of completed tasks;
- **proficient** is able to predict, either intuitively or analytically, what would be expected with new tasks;
- **expert** can define not only what would be expected with new types of work, but will be able to identify what the impact will be on other areas of the business and where potential problems are likely to arise.

Using this classification, your company can define its own skills profile. The two extremes are the normal pyramid and the inverted pyramid (Figure 2.4).

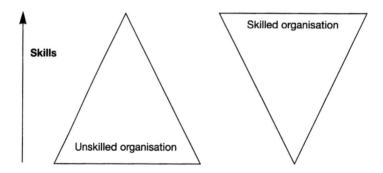

Fig. 2.4 Structure of unskilled and skilled organisations

Increasing skills allows the company to carry out more complex and demanding strategies. Studies have shown that the more highly skilled the organisation, the higher its medium-term profitability. Companies can set a target for skills levels – moving from an average of 2.5, for example (the company with a level of skill between advanced beginner and competent), to 3.1 (between competent and proficient). It is applied in Chapter 9 in the business health check.

Setting objectives for skills development has significant effects on the way the organisation behaves. It improves training, recruitment and motivational policies within the company.

⟱ **High levels of skills mean higher long-term profits and increased flexibility within the business culture.**

Understanding the current position of these key objectives and considering what possible targets can be set is an important issue in establishing whether or not the plan is realistic and attainable (see Table 2.2).

Table 2.2   Checklist of specific objectives

Objective	Current	Possible
1. Improving gross profit levels		
2. Controlling fixed costs		
3. In control of new product development		
4. Using advantages of increasing skills level		

PAST SUCCESSES AND FAILURES

All businesses can learn from the past years' trading history – what they attempted to achieve, why they succeeded or why they failed and what, with the value of hindsight, they should have done. Each business will have different dynamics, but Table 2.3 is a standard checklist (much of this is used again in the health check in Chapter 9).

- **Customer base**   Have we maintained the existing customer base or managed to achieve growth?
- **Area**   Did we achieve the coverage of the area we planned to?
- **Sales volumes**   Have we achieved the targeted sales volumes?
- **Margins**   Have we achieved our target profit levels?
- **New product development**   Did we achieve what we expected from new product or new service development?

- **Productivity**   Did we achieve our planned level of output per employee?
- **Skills level**   Did we manage to build on the skills base within the organisation?
- **Fixed costs**   Were our fixed costs in line with our expectations?
- **Suppliers**   Were the suppliers meeting our sales requirements?
- **Information systems**   Did we have the information necessary to control the business?

At this stage, the emphasis remains on broad areas and objectives – the detailed 'How?'s of achieving change can be kept for later in the plan – but we must still, now, identify exact areas of concern.

Table 2.3   Checklist of successes and failures

Factor	Achievement percentage	Reason	What to do
Customer base			
Area			
Sales volumes			
Margins			
New product development			
Productivity			
Skills level			
Fixed costs			
Suppliers			
Information systems			

Throughout the book, two examples of SMEs are described to show how the concepts introduced can be applied in practice.

CASE STUDY   **Softawater, part I**

Softawater is a manufacturing company that produces water softeners. The product range consists of three tabletop systems, *Alpha*, *Beta* and *Gamma*, one small industrial system, *Delta*, and one large industrial system, *Omega*.

The company was established five years ago by three ex-employees of a German water treatment company. The backgrounds of these three people, directors of Softawater, are as follows.

- George Graham, 52, has an engineering background. He has worked since the age of 16 within the water treatment industry. His main enthusiasms are for solving technical problems and meeting production targets.
- Diane Flowers, 43, has an accounting qualification. Diane is divorced with three young children. Her main motivations are the potential security provided by her shareholding and the existing success of the business.
- David Matra, 38, has a sales background. David is the risk taker of the three, with continual ideas about expansion and growth.

There is a workforce of 30 and the production plant is some of the most modern in Europe.

The market for water softeners is steadily expanding throughout Europe in line with a demand for higher-quality water from a stressed public water system. The company had expanded slowly over the first five years, and now has a stable customer base spread over a fairly large geographic area.

Setting general objectives

The three directors have first established where they stand on the main personal/general objectives of the business (see Table 2.4). This shows that there is some disagreement – with directors in clear dispute over the potential loss of control, and level of risk that will be acceptable in the future development of the firm.

Table 2.4   Softawater's completed checklist of general objectives

Objectives	Completely agree	Largely agree	Agree but with little enthusiasm	Disagree	Violently disagree
1. Do we want to grow?	DM	GG, DF			
2. Perspective long or short term?	DM, GG, DF				
3. Do we want new challenges?	DM, GG		DF		
4. Do we want to maintain control?	GG			DF	DM
5. High earnings vital?	DM	DF		GG	
6. Will we risk all?	DM		GG	DF	

Timescale

Softawater is a light engineering company. Typically, it will take a year for a product to be designed and put into production, with an 18-month pay-back period. The directors therefore propose to establish a three-year planning cycle, with a detailed plan for next year, including all targets quantified by area, followed by outline projections that will be updated every three months as the plan develops.

Key objectives

Softawater is a business that has historically achieved good profit margins, although fixed costs have risen steadily during the last five years (Table 2.5). The company has not had a solid record of new product development, and the skills level has remained below the industry average.

From the existing position, the directors consider that a new range of performance indicators can be established that will be consistent with their agreed general goals and objectives.

Table 2.5   Softawater's completed checklist of specific objectives

Objectives	Current achievement	Possible target
1. Gross profit	33%	30–39%
2. Fixed costs	£360k	£330–380k
3. New product numbers	1	2–3
4. Skills level	2.8	2.7–3.2

The company assessed, on an initial quick evaluation, that its main problems are in new product development and the production department (Table 2.6).

Table 2.6   Softawater's completed checklist of successes and failures

Factor	Achievement percentage	Reason	What to do
Customer base	80	Poor promotion	Change policy
Area	105	Sales team	Continue
Sales volumes	85	Product/competition	New product development
Margins	75	Pricing OK, but production costs up	New equipment/ better planning
New product development	30	Management	Change personnel
Productivity	64	Work planning	Improve
Skills level	55	Training programme	Change
Fixed costs	102	Cost control programme	Continue
Suppliers	70	Poor quality/delivery	New suppliers
Information systems	100	Management	Continue

Brainstorm, part I

Brainstorm is a toy retailer, established ten years ago by husband and wife David and Marjorie Allingham. The initial store has expanded to three within a 50-mile radius. The company specialises in a wide range of educational toys, which it buys from a large number of suppliers. Where it differs from other retailers is in its approach to the market, with an emphasis on creating a network of contacts within the local education sector via presentations to specific interest groups, such as parent-teacher associations, special educational needs groups and so on.

David and Marjorie are now 58 and 52 respectively. Their children have left home and do not want to join their parents in the business.

The company employs ten staff in addition to the directors, who are actively managing stores on a rota basis.

General objectives

The analysis of the general objectives reveals a much lower level of commitment to growth, expansion and risk from the two owners of the business (Table 2.7).

Table 2.7   Brainstorm's completed checklist of general objectives

Objectives	Completely agree	Largely agree	Agree but with little enthusiasm	Disagree	Violently disagree
1. Do we want to grow?			DA, MA		
2. Perspective long or short term?			MA	DA	
3. Do we want new challenges?				DA, MA	
4. Do we want to maintain control?	DA, MA				
5. High earnings vital?				DA, MA	
6. Will we risk all?					DA, MA

Timescale

The company considers that, realistically, it would take two years to open a new store and achieve an adequate level of payback, and it has chosen this timescale for its plan. Within a two-year period, short-term goals are the next six months, medium-term goals are the following year and long-term goals the final six months.

Key objectives

Brainstorm has always achieved fair profit margins, although the local area has become more competitive with similar chains entering the market (see Table 2.8). A significant proportion of their stock has historically consisted of new lines as the educational market is continually changing. Fixed costs tend to be fairly static on a store-by-store basis, although expansion would inevitably lead to an increase in this area. Skills levels remain a problem – the company failing to maintain effective skills among its other store employees.

Table 2.8 Brainstorm's completed checklist of specific objectives

Objectives	Current achievement	Possible target
1. Gross profit	50%	46–52%
2. Fixed costs	£130k	£130–180k
3. New product numbers	30%	30%
4. Skills level	2.3	2.3–2.5

Successes and failures

Brainstorm's directors consider that, in the previous year, they have achieved the majority of their objectives (Table 2.9). However there have been problems with suppliers and sales – which are connected with the failure to adequately service all the special interest groups outside the retail outlets. This has also meant that the area covered by the chain has been smaller than was anticipated.

Table 2.9 Brainstorm's completed checklist of successes and failures

Factor	Achievement percentage	Reason	What to do
Customer base	85	Poor interest group contact	Create new programme
Area	70	Same as above	
Sales volumes	95	Impact of interest group contact	
Margins	103	Better product mix	Continue
New product development	85	Supplier shortfall	Search for new suppliers
Productivity	80	Staff sickness	Recruit part-timers
Skills level	85	Staff lacks skills for interest groups	Train
Fixed costs	100	Controlled	
Suppliers policy	77	Deliveries	New buying policy
Information systems	80	Lack of product sales information	New software

The company has also experienced other problems with suppliers and the information system, which needs adjustment and improvement.

SUMMARY

This chapter has discussed the important broad issues that must be clarified at the earliest possible stage in the development of the business plan. These were separated into general objectives and key quantifiable and specific objectives, which contribute to the assumptions on which the plan is based and will be re-appraised and fine-tuned in Chapters 8 and 9. To help the SME, a practical, simple approach to identifying these broad issues has been provided.

SMEs can learn from past experience, and becoming familiar with uncomplicated techniques for identifying strengths and weaknesses is essential planning information.

Because planning places objectives within a time frame, a simple method of deciding on the appropriate timescale was described, based on new product development time.

The concept of success and failure analysis was introduced as SMEs can learn from past experience, and becoming familiar with uncomplicated techniques for identifying strengths and weaknesses is essential planning information. The subject of strengths and weakness analysis is returned to in Chapter 5.

The information system – the foundation of successful planning

INTRODUCTION

You can use planning to move forward only if you know where you are to start with:

- where your business is currently;
- how you can improve its performance;
- where it should be going.

This and the chapters that follow deal with each of these in turn, in a systematic and structured way.

You can solve a problem only if you first recognise that it exists. An information system provides the detail about the current state of the business

You can solve a problem only if you first recognise that it exists. An information system provides the detail about the current state of the business and this serves as the foundation of the business planning exercise.

and this serves as the foundation of the business planning exercise. Information gives you a competitive advantage as most of the competing SMEs will have limited or non-existent information systems.

⇨ **Always start a business plan from a clear appreciation of the current state of the business.**

This chapter familiarises the SME planner with a variety of information system techniques that, taken together, give a clear view of the detailed, current state of the business. But as you proceed, always remember that every business is in some ways unique and therefore has different information requirements and so the information system developed and used must take account of these differences.

POINTS TO THINK ABOUT

An information system helps in the running of the business by identifying – and therefore helping to resolve – problems, and in making the SME aware of new opportunities. For the SME with a limited number of personnel, correctly identifying what information to collect and maintain is vital. Too much unnecessary information often means that none that is essential will be collected, while collecting too little will mean that many of the important control issues in the business will be missed.

A related issue in building an effective information system is flexibility – recognising that the different information needs of each business will change over time as new policies are developed and new initiatives pursued.

So, an information system must be managed. It should not be allowed to manage, otherwise it will become an end in itself and will not serve the company. For example, many manufacturers should monitor the effectiveness of their distribution systems, as they make up such a large proportion of their costs. As distribution costs are allocated under a variety of headings in off-the-shelf information systems, the management of this area of the business requires some thought and rearrangement of the way in which the information is collected as the business develops.

⇨ **Develop an information system that gives you the information you need, not what another provider thinks you need.**

MANAGING THE INFORMATION SYSTEM

Decisions have to be made about the following:

- the frequency with which information is collected and analysed;
- who to assign to the planning and monitoring team, which will develop the plan, implement it and monitor it as it develops;
- developing role models for success against which the performance of the business can be measured as the plan is built up – known as benchmarking, which is discussed later in this chapter;
- who should have access to the information.

■ The frequency of information reviews

Each business must decide how it will review and use the information collected and try to formalise the procedures adopted.

Ideally, the management system should consist of:

- control information that is collected and used frequently, either weekly or every two weeks;
- intermittent information, which is collected and reviewed every month or two months;
- planning information, which is used to update the plan and identify major changes in the business environment.

For the SME, these fine concepts must be modified to take account of the fact that its managers are normally busy with the day-to-day affairs of the company and have limited time to devote to review and planning issues.

It is sensible in most cases to manage the key issue – cash flow – on a daily or weekly basis and the others monthly. Most banks and outside financial supporters expect the completion of the profit and loss account by the third week in the month, and it therefore makes sense to hold the review meeting concerning the previous month's figures at the end of the third week of the month.

■ Creating the planning team

For many SMEs, the concept of a planning and information collection *team* may cause wry smiles of amusement. However, even in the smallest company there are normally individuals with general responsibilities for the key planning and control areas. Part of the value of the planning process may be to formalise these responsibilities and crystallise a reporting structure that can be integrated into the future level of control the company obtains from the business plan.

Staff need to be identified who will have responsibility for collecting planning information in a number of areas:

- product and customer development – sales and marketing;
- production and/or customer service – production;

- cost and cash control – finance;
- personnel development and integration – managing director;
- new product development – product development director.

Once the planning and information collection team has been created, some form of fairly detailed schedule should be adopted so that a target date for the completion of the plan can be approximated. For a company of any size, three planning periods are normally sensible.

Completion of information system	Date	Responsibility
First forecast	Date	Responsibility
Second revisions	Date	Responsibility
Final plan	Date	Responsibility

Remember that involving staff in the development and implementation of the business plan is one of the most effective ways of identifying individuals who can be promoted. Whoever is chosen, it is vital that the same individuals are responsible for developing the plan, implementing and monitoring the results. It is impossible to gain commitment and involvement with the plan unless those who plan are also those who implement.

⇨ **Use the planning team to develop the plan, implement it and monitor it.**

■ Learning from others – benchmarking

Many companies – even those not in the same sector – face similar problems, but some are able to exploit the same opportunities better than others. What are these companies doing that makes them so special and effective?

At each stage of the market analysis of the major forces acting on the company, the business planner needs to consider how other companies have handled the problem or exploited the opportunity – a process known as benchmarking. Although benchmarking is normally associated with positive performance, it is often as valuable to consider firms that are carrying out an activity particularly badly. This is because knowing what *not* to do is often as useful (or in some instances more useful) as knowing what to do. In this chapter, benchmarks are given in the case studies to help illustrate their value.

Although benchmarking is normally associated with positive performance, it is often as valuable to consider firms that are carrying out an activity particularly badly. This is because knowing what not to do is often as useful (or in some instances more useful) as knowing what to do.

■ Who should have access to the information?

The final decision managers and business planners need to make about an information system is who has access to the information collected.

Research indicates a strong link between information and profitability. The more information provided, the higher the level of profitability. There are normally two main reasons put forward for this – better decision making and motivation. First, the larger the numbers making a contribution, the better the decision. Second, wider access to information reduces friction as individuals are clear about what is occurring and how their input is being integrated into the overall direction of the company.

In practical terms, for most SMEs, this will mean a far greater use of the noticeboard or, where the firm is computerised, the creation of an internal electronic bulletin board. For most companies it makes sense to display:

- profit and loss figures;
- order book;
- major new contracts;
- new products.

▷ **Distribute information widely to build company loyalty and involvement.**

KEY CONTROL ELEMENTS IN THE INFORMATION SYSTEM

Having emphasised from the beginning that each business has its own special information requirements, it must also be said that what does not differ is the way in which this information is presented. Think of it as being similar to a doctor's case notes: the details for each patient will be different, but the form the case notes take will not.

For each business, there are eight key control elements in the information system:

- cash flow;
- profit and loss statement;
- balance sheet;
- financial ratios;
- production/service supply efficiencies;
- new product/service supply development efficiencies;
- personnel efficiencies;
- marketing efficiencies.

The exact information included under each of these headings should be tailored to the requirements of each business, though some of them will be influenced by the information-gathering procedure. Thus, the computer software used for accounting in almost all businesses today provides a template for the profit and loss statement, the balance sheet and the way in which financial ratios are calculated. Production ratios and controls are largely superfluous in a service company; although personnel and marketing controls are likely to be relevant in all profit-based businesses.

■ Cash flow

Cash flow is a forecast of how money will move through the business. It includes an analysis of orders or prospective sales, the income from those sales and any other payments, and how money will move out of the business in the form of pay, expenditure on premises, materials and other services.

An accurate cash flow model enables the SME to assess the impact of additional business, rises in raw material and labour costs, changes in payment speeds – a whole series of 'What if ...?'s.

Cash is king – a company with a positive cash flow can pay its bills, invest in developing the business and move forward. It should form the basis of all business plans, with the planning team starting the process of working out a cash flow forecast for the planning horizon.

➡️ **Cash flow forecasts are the backbone of any business plan.**

An accurate cash flow statement also helps the company control the business on a day-to-day or week-to-week basis, by providing a crucial short-term monitoring system. This means that, for the SME, the cash flow defines what short-term information the company needs to maintain effective control.

It is important to remember that cash flow is dealing with the immediate activity of the business, and that income and expenditure will not relate directly to each other. For example, a sale in month 2 may have incurred labour costs in month 1, and material costs in month 2, but will not be received as income until month 3. A cash flow needs to take account of this by reference to phasing the payments in, and out, by reference to the relevant credit obtained from suppliers and the credit the SME has to provide to its customers. As the business expands, or introduces new products, it spends money in advance of receiving its return – negative cash flow. Equally there will be periods when more money is coming in than is going out – positive cash flow.

Whether to include or exclude certain items in the cash flow is for company management to decide. The cash flow can, for example, include sales tax (VAT) payments, or not.

Forecasting is a central part of cash flow – identifying trends in orders, prices and costs. The complexity of the forecasting system depends on the environment in which a particular SME operates. Where it has stable, repeatable business, forecasting of the future can be built on previous experience. Where the environment is volatile, more complicated forecasting methods are required. For the business developing a plan, these forecasting systems are of paramount importance, and expertise in using them will become a vital skill.

Every forecast made is subject to a certain level of risk. Some of these risks are small, others large. The greater the level of risk involved in the forecast, the greater the investment required in time and money (in the shape of investment in forecasting systems) to improve the control the business is able to exert. The company can reduce levels of risk by taking steps, such as agreeing contracts with major customers and major suppliers that guarantee the volume and cost of sales and raw materials. But an element of risk will always remain. Major risk components must be noted down as crucial assumptions in the plan.

A number of forecasting methods are available. With the reduced costs of computer software, companies have greater access to the more sophisticated methods than before. The main options are listed in Table 3.1.

Table 3.1　Forecasting methods and implications for timescales

Type	Advantages	Disadvantages	Timescales
Straight line	Quick, easy	Only works where no fluctuation exists	Very short term
Moving total	Quick to calculate Smooths seasonality	Does not identify market change, or relationships	Short term
Exponential smoothing	Easy to calculate deals with major market change	Does not identify market relationships	Short to medium term
Time series analysis	Now wide range of computer software Identifies market relationships	Needs good data	Medium term
Econometric modelling	Identifies external factors that drive sales	Modelling expensive, needs good data	Long term
Scenario building	Provides detailed model of environment	Very expensive, needs high-class data	Long term

Softawater, part II

- **Sales**   Softawater uses its customer categorisation as a basis for the start of its cash flow analysis (see Table 3.2). Customers A and B are two of the large supermarket groups. Customer C is the major wholesaler used by the company to service the smaller outlets. D customers are small industrial companies and E customers are the larger.
- **Revenue**   All customers pay within 30 days, which means that the sales in the previous month are reflected in the revenue of the following month.
- **Other income** reflects the slow growth of overseas sales to Holland and Belgium, and a small training grant that the company received in the current year. Total income is the combination of the various sales lines.
- **Raw materials** for Softawater are the chemicals that fill the consumer products and the plastic granules that are converted to make the casing for the table unit and the filtration system.
- **Subcontracted materials and components** are those that are purchased for the industrial units. Softawater holds the design patents on these products, but only carries out the assembly of the parts in-house.
- Most of the **labour** employed by Softawater is paid a fixed monthly salary, but occasionally temporary staff are hired on a piece-work basis to cover particular peaks in production during the summer.
- **Energy** used directly in production is accounted for via meters attached to the equipment.
- **Distribution costs**   Packaging and transport are included as part of the variable cost expenditure.
- **Premises** are the costs of the company plant and the property taxes.
- **New product development** costs are entered in their own section in order to identify the investment needed for the creation of the target number of new products.

Softawater could use historic information to develop a longer-term forecasting model. By building up the company on a customer-by-customer basis, the company could create a fairly clear picture of what the medium-term trends are likely to be, although the underlying growth in the market means that these forecasts would need to be modified.

Table 3.2   Softawater's cash flow analysis (£000)

Items	Month											
	1	2	3	4	5	6	7	8	9	10	11	12
Sales:												
Customer A	100	150	120	130	120	110	100	90	150	180	200	150
Customer B	180	170	140	110	120	160	140	130	110	150	250	200
Customer C	250	200	210	200	240	260	280	300	340	360	380	300
Customer D	200	120	110	90	70	60	100	120	130	150	170	180
Customer E												
Total sales	630	650	580	530	550	590	620	640	730	840	1000	830
Revenue	800	630	650	580	530	550	590	620	640	730	840	1000
Other income			50			100			150			
Total inflow	800	630	700	580	530	650	590	620	790	730	840	1000
Raw materials	180	163	165	158	153	155	159	162	164	173	184	200
Subcontract	20	15	15	15	15	12	15	15	15	16	17	20
Labour	5	5							10	5	5	5
Utilities	10	10	8	8	8	8	8	10	10	10	10	10
Logistics	16	15	15	15	12	12	15	15	16	18	20	25
Variable flow costs	569	422	497	384	382	363	393	418	575	508	594	740
Premises	35	35	35	35	35	35	35	35	35	35	35	35
Pay – staff	170	170	170	170	170	170	170	170	170	170	170	170
Pay – administration	100	100	100	100	100	100	100	100	100	100	100	100
Professional	3	3	3	3	3	3	3	3	3	3	3	3
Travel	3	3	3	3	3	3	3	3	3	3	3	3
Promotion	15	15	15	15	15	15	15	15	15	15	15	15
Utilities	5	5	5	5	5	5	5	5	5	5	5	5
Equipment cost	10	10	10	10	10	10	10	10	10	10	10	10
New product development	20	20	20	20	20	20	20	20	20	20	20	20
Miscellaneous	3	3	3	3	3	3	3	3	3	3	3	3
Finance costs	55	55	55	55	55	55	55	55	55	55	55	55
Fixed costs	419	419	419	419	419	419	419	419	419	419	419	419
Total flow	150	3	78	(33)	(37)	(56)	(36)	19	156	89	175	321
Opening bank	100	250	253	331	298	261	206	170	189	345	434	609
Closing bank	250	253	331	298	261	206	170	189	345	434	609	930

45

Most of the costs the company incurs could be forecast by looking at prior experience (historic data). Raw material costs vary with the underlying cost of petroleum products, so these could be forecast on the basis of figures supplied by the industry with a fair degree of success, and low level of risk. The cost of premises is fixed for the next five years, pay will move in line with the industry average, and distribution costs are fixed by contract with outside suppliers.

What has always been a major area of uncertainty is the cost of new product development. The company has invested heavily in this over the past years without creating any effective new products in the industrial sector. This means that either the process has been ineffective or that insufficient resources have been made available to the programme.

Benchmark

Softawater has not managed to gain access to comparable company information, against which it could analyse its cash flow system. It is aware, however, that some other companies have used factoring agents to speed their revenue flows, that other companies have been paying substantially less for their finance and that many have used outside agencies for their new product development.

CASE STUDY **Brainstorm, part II**

Brainstorm, by contrast, has a much simpler cash flow management system (see Table 3.3).

- **Customers** are divided into four categories: special interest groups, such as parent-teacher associations, learning difficulty groups, are classified as A customers; primary schools and pre-school groups as B customers; secondary schools as C customers; sales via the retail stores, and other means, mainly mail order, as D customers.
- **Total sales** is the combination of these four categories.
- **Inflow** is always within the month of the sale – even for those purchases made by credit card, which account for 60 per cent of retail sales.
- **Stock purchases** are paid for, in theory, 60 days after delivery, but, in reality, payment terms are generally much shorter.
- **Casual labour** is hired for busy periods of the year, with 50 per cent of sales being achieved during the months of November and December.

- **Premises** are the combined cost of all outlets and property taxes.
- **Pay** is the salaries of all regular employees and the directors.

Forecasts could be created based on this historic data and have a fair degree of accuracy. Each customer category would purchase a defined value of products – parent-teacher associations of primary schools, for example, purchasing 40 per cent more goods by value than secondary school parent-teacher associations. Costs are similarly well understood and most are fixed in the medium term.

Table 3.3   Brainstorm's cash flow analysis (£000)

Items	Month											
	1	2	3	4	5	6	7	8	9	10	11	12
Sales: A customers	20	10	10	20	10	10	20	30	40	40	40	20
B customers	10	20	20	30	40	10	20	10	10	10	10	10
C customers	5	5	5	5	5				5	5	5	5
D customers												
Retail	120	120	130	140	120	110	100	180	200	250	300	250
Other			5		5		5		5			
Total sales	155	155	170	195	180	130	155	220	260	305	355	285
Total inflow	155	155	170	195	180	130	155	220	260	305	355	285
Stock purchases	45	45	50	58	54	40	45	84	78	90	106	85
Casual labour								10	10	10	10	10
Variable costs	45	45	50	58	54	40	45	94	88	100	116	95
Premises	50	50	50	50	50	50	50	50	50	50	50	50
Pay	30	30	30	30	30	30	30	30	30	30	30	30
Promotion	3	3	3	3	3	3	3	5	5	5	5	5
Utilities	2	2	2	2	2	2	2	2	2	2	2	2
Professional	2	2	2	2	2	2	2	2	2	2	2	2
Finance charges	3	3	3	3	3	3	3	3	3	3	3	3
Fixed flow	90	90	90	90	90	90	90	92	92	92	92	92
Net flow	20	20	30	67	36	0	20	34	90	153	239	108
Opening bank	70	90	110	140	207	243	243	263	297	387	540	779
Closing bank	90	110	140	207	243	243	263	297	387	540	779	887

Benchmark

Brainstorm does not have access to comparable company data. From what the directors have managed to learn from other companies in the local district, they are not making sufficient use of direct bank payments to the utility companies, which would further reduce their utility cost by improving their level of discount.

■ Profit and loss

The profit and loss statement evaluates the total level of sales (not actual income), the cost of those sales and the profit generated on those sales. It includes depreciation, which is a non-cash item, and where the company writes off bad debts. The profit and loss statement compares the position in the current month with the year to date. It is sensible to use the same categories in establishing the profit and loss as are present in the cash flow.

■ *Costing methods*

The way in which a business costs sales has important consequences for how its information system works.

This book favours a clear distinction between costs that vary according to the volume of product or service (variable costs) and those which have to be incurred regardless of the level of production (fixed costs). Choosing which are variable costs and which are fixed is a matter to be decided by each business. The distinction used in this book is that of considering most labour as fixed – businesses that are building skills cannot hire and fire arbitrarily. Similarly, promotion, equipment, finance and new product development costs are included as fixed costs as they are investments that have to be made in the development of the business.

The advantage of this costing approach is that it clearly separates out those costs that the firm needs to continually incur, and provides a true indication of where the breakeven point of the business will lie (see Figure 2.2, page 23). However, the whole area of costing is one of the most hotly debated topics in certain business circles and any costing approach has its problems – as does this, when certain products take more time or use more space to produce than others.

Variable costs
- Raw materials, components
- Part-time labour
- Logistics
- Utility cost relating to production

Fixed costs
- Rent, rates
- Full-time labour
- Sales and promotion
- New product development
- Finance
- Equipment
- Utility
- Professional services

Softawater, part III

At the end of the year, Softawater has overcome the poor profitability of the first three months, as higher volumes feed through the fixed cost base. Most of the cost centres have not increased out of line with the increased volumes, and the company, for example, has had much lower logistics/ distribution costs than its competitors, and spent less heavily on sales and promotion.

The company has chosen to use a conservative approach in managing its profit and loss account, writing off all product development costs as they have occurred and bad debts three months after the payment was due (see Table 3.4). It has also depreciated equipment at the most rapid rate possible.

Benchmark
Softawater has been able to use its competitors' published figures to analyse their profit and loss and where they have been successful. Aqua spent much more heavily on sales and promotion, on professional fees and had a higher bad debt ratio.

The main industrial waste management company, Pura, has consistently spent more heavily on new product development than Softawater.

Table 3.4   Softawater's profit and loss statement (£000)

Items	Month 12	Year to date
Sales	830	8490
Stock purchases (net)	220	2506
Direct labour	5	45
Utilities	10	110
Distribution costs	20	184
Gross profit	575	5645
%	69	66
Premises	35	400
Pay – production	170	2040
Pay – administration	100	1200
Equipment	10	120
Utilities	5	60
Travel	3	36
New product development	20	240
Promotion	15	180
Professional	3	36
Depreciation	7	85
Bad debts	5	30
Finance	55	660
Misc	3	40
Net profit	280	821
%	33	9.6

Brainstorm, part III

Brainstorm has been consistently profitable over the last three years, with profits rising as margins have been improved as a result of its new products unavailable in other outlets (see Table 3.5). The company has also benefited from its strong cash position, which has enabled it to handle seasonal problems without a substantial effect on its profitability.

Benchmark

Brainstorm has noted that many of its competitors spend far more heavily on promotion and pay, with directors' fees making up a considerable proportion of the total pay bill in many other companies.

Table 3.5   Brainstorm's profit and loss statement (£000)

Items	Month 12	Year to date
Sales	285	2565
Stock purchases (net)	85	870
Direct labour	10	50
Gross profit	190	1645
%	66	64
Premises	50	600
Pay	30	360
Utilities	2	24
Promotion	5	46
Professional	2	24
Bad debts	–	–
Finance	3	36
Net profit	98	555
%	34	21

■ Balance sheet

The balance sheet gives the assets and liabilities of a company and the various categories of assets, whether they can be easily liquidated or can be called on rapidly. It also takes account of the depreciation and appreciation of assets during the accounting period, changes in the levels of stocks, work in progress, debtors and creditors, reductions in outstanding loans and so on.

CASE STUDY ## Softawater, part IV

Softawater has continued to see an increase in its cash balances towards the end of the year, although the increased level of sales in the final few months has meant that a higher level of activity has had to be funded via the debtor book and more stock and work in progress (see Table 3.6).

Equipment purchases have continued to outstrip the impact of depreciation so that for every month during the year, there has been a net increase in the total equipment value. The high levels of equipment purchase have meant that the company has borrowed substantially to re-equip the factory.

Benchmark

A number of other companies seem to have been more effective in managing their balance sheets. Some lease their equipment, others have a higher level of equity participation and a lower level of loans. All have had a higher creditor ratio than Softawater does.

....

Table 3.6   Softawater's balance sheet (£000)

Items	Current month (12)	Year to date
Fixed assets		
Equipment	10	470
Premises	–	40
Total fixed assets	10	510
Current assets		
Stock and work in progress	28	1110
Debtors	15	830
Cash	280	880
Total current assets	223	2910
Current liabilities		
Creditors	5	430
Bank	–	–
Loans up to 1 year	25	250
Tax	23	85
Total current liabilities	58	765
Net current assets over net liabilities	270	2145
Total assets over liabilities	280	2655
Financed by:		
Equity	–	250
Profit and loss	280	1905
Loans over 1 year	–	500

Brainstorm, part IV

The growth in profitability of the company over the past years has not been accompanied by the need to fund extremely high levels of stock or debtors. The business is primarily a cash one with customers paying by cheque or by credit card, both of which generate payment quickly. The tax position is becoming difficult for the company as a result of the improved profitability.

Management has decided not to value the leases on its four shops or the value of the shopfittings and other equipment in the stores. The directors are of the view that these would have no value should the stores cease trading and so have not included them on a conservative basis (see Table 3.7).

Benchmark

Brainstorm is well placed compared with major competitors. The main weakness appears to have been the limited use it has made of creditor finance.

■ Financial ratios

The profit and loss statement and the balance sheet provide the business with the ability to analyse a whole range of important ratios, which are valuable measures of the underlying health of the operation and where there are problems that need to be acted on.

Ratios have traditionally been divided into three main categories:

■ **profitability ratios**, which measure profitability and returns on sales (in Chapter 2, the gross profit ratio was used as part of the search for specific quantifiable objectives);

■ **activity ratios**, which measure how a company is using its money as it trades;

■ **liquidity ratios**, which measure the ability of the company to pay its debts.

The relevance of the financial and other ratios will become clearer when, in other chapters, the short- and long-term options for action are considered.

Table 3.7   Brainstorm's balance sheet (£000)

Items	Current month (12)	Year to date
Fixed assets		
Equipment	–	–
Premises	–	–
Total fixed assets	–	–
Current assets		
Stock and work in progress	15	320
Debtors	2	35
Cash	100	750
Total current assets	117	1105
Current liabilities		
Creditors	8	85
Bank	–	–
Loans up to 1 year	–	–
Tax	11	155
Total current liabilities	33	240
Net current assets over net liabilities	98	780
Financed by:		
Equity	–	100
Profit and loss	98	680
Loans	–	–

■ Profitability ratios

Gross profit ratio (GPR)

Gross profit is generally considered to be the profit before the operating and administrative expenses have been deducted. Some companies call it gross profit after factory indirects (GPAFI). It is the measure of the mark-up on goods sold.

$$GPR = \frac{\text{price of sale} - \text{cost of sale}}{\text{price of sale}/100}$$

This ratio is one of the key factors in managing the company – higher gross profit margins being crucial to company success. Declining gross profit margins can result from:

- a poorer product mix;
- a poorer-quality product that is unable to command reasonable prices;
- higher costs of sales;
- a more competitive marketplace, demanding keener prices;
- sales representative failure, providing too high a level of discount.

Net profit ratio (NPR)

This is the profit the company is making after the deduction of all expenses not directly associated with the cost of production. Allocating expenses between those directly concerned with production and those that are not is often thought of as something of a black art.

$$NPR = \frac{\text{total sales} - \text{cost of sale} - \text{all other costs}}{\text{price of sale}/100}$$

Declining net profit margins may be caused by:

- lower sales volumes;
- lower gross profit margins (see above);
- higher indirect costs.

Return on total assets or return on capital employed (ROCE)

The total assets employed in the business are premises and equipment, debtors, stock and work in progress and cash in hand, less liabilities, which are creditors, loans.

$$ROCE = \frac{\text{net profit before tax and loan interest}}{\text{total assets}/100}$$

Return on capital employed is a general measure of the effectiveness of every company. Successful ones generate return on capital employed ratios in excess of 20 per cent year-on-year, while unsuccessful ones have ratios of under 10 per cent.

Declining returns on capital employed suggest problems with:

- gross margins;
- net margins;
- management of fixed assets;
- increasing current assets – stock in particular.

Breakeven ratio

Control of fixed costs was an issue in the setting of quantifiable specific objectives in Chapter 2 (Figure 2.2). SMEs need to be continually aware of the relationship between the profit they are generating per unit sold and the underlying fixed cost structure. The formula for calculating breakeven value is repeated here so you have a complete set of ratios.

$$BEV = \frac{\text{fixed costs}}{\text{margin per unit}}$$

Changing breakeven values are obviously caused by:

- increases in fixed costs;
- declining volumes;
- reduced profitability per unit.

Activity ratios

Stock turnover ratio (STR)

The faster the stock turnover every year, the more efficient the business will be, subject to the overall service objectives of the firm. Stock turnover needs to be very high in companies operating on low margins (wholesalers and certain retailers, for example), but can be substantially lower in companies with high margins (such as antique shops).

$$STR = \frac{\text{sales}}{\text{average stock value}}$$

Poor stock turnover ratios suggest:

- poor product mix;
- increasing levels of obsolescent stock;
- poor control of the ordering of raw materials;
- poor control of work in progress.

Working capital ratio (WCR)

The working capital ratio provides a measure of how the company will need to fund extra sales, and of the efficiency with which it manages both current assets and current liabilities.

$$\text{WCR} = \frac{\text{working capital (current assets} - \text{current liabilities)}}{\text{sales}/100}$$

The working capital ratio also provides a useful measure of what financing would be required to expand, providing all elements making up the working capital ratio continued to behave in the same fashion. Remember that this may not be the case; changing company direction may mean holding greater levels of stock, and work in progress and new projects may mean that new suppliers have to be paid in advance.

High working capital ratios can be attributed to:

- poor stock turnover ratio;
- poor control of debtors;
- poor control of creditors.

Sales expense ratio (SER)

This ratio measures the cost of sales against the overall sales expenditure level and provides a method of controlling sales expenses:

$$\text{SER} = \frac{\text{sales expenses}}{\text{sales}/100}$$

A rising sales expense ratio may be due to one or several factors, including:

- a more widely spread customer base – due to foreign travel, for example;
- a significant rise in the number of customers;

- increased numbers of sales representatives;
- higher levels of expenditure per call;
- increased management costs in the salesforce;
- rising pay costs.

Again, this ratio is relevant to the discussion of short-term actions taken to deal with such problems in fine-tuning sales in Chapter 4.

Administration expense ratio (AER)

Similarly, companies can monitor the level of administrative overhead:

$$AER = \frac{\text{administration expenses}}{\text{sales}/100}$$

A rising administration expense ratio can be caused by one or a number of factors, including:

- rising pay costs of staff;
- increased workload because of larger account base;
- a larger number of supervisory management appointments.

Debtor ratio (DR)

The debtor ratio analyses how long customers take to pay their bills.

$$DR = \frac{\text{total average debtors}}{\text{total sales}/365}$$

The debtor ratio is a measure of the effectiveness of the credit control process. The following may be responsible for poor debtor ratios:

- extended credit periods for customers;
- poor credit control;
- quality control problems, leading to customer complaints;
- invoicing problems.

Creditor ratio (CR)

The creditor ratio provides a measure of how much credit is being taken from suppliers:

$$CR = \frac{\text{total average creditors}}{\text{total sales}/365}$$

A worsening creditor ratio is a sign that the company is not being as effective as it should in obtaining credit. The causes might be:

- a poor history of meeting previous credit terms;
- a failure to negotiate effectively with suppliers on credit.

Bad debt ratio (BDR)

Bad debts can, and do, kill companies. The management of potential bad debts is one of the key issues in company planning, especially when the business is expanding or changing direction.

$$BDR = \frac{\text{bad debts}}{\text{total sales}}$$

A rising bad debt ratio can be caused by one or more of several factors, including:

- lack of clearly defined credit limits for each customer;
- poor ongoing credit control;
- failure to check creditworthiness prior to opening new accounts.

■ Liquidity ratios

These provide various measures of how easily a company can pay its debts.

Current ratio (CR)

The current ratio provides a measure of whether or not a company is still technically liquid.

$$CR = \frac{\text{current assets}}{\text{current liabilities}}$$

Ratios below 1 mean that the company is technically insolvent. The legislation concerning insolvency means that directors of the company need to monitor this ratio carefully to ensure that it remains above 1.

When the current ratio is declining, there is a need to either increase the current assets or – often more realistic – reduce current liabilities by converting loans and the like into equity, thus reducing liabilities and improving the debt to equity ratio (see overleaf).

Quick ratio (QR)

The quick ratio analyses the ability of the business to pay its way on a day-to-day basis by excluding the stock and work in progress from the calculation of the current assets that are available to service creditors:

$$QR = \frac{\text{current assets} - (\text{stock and work in progress})}{\text{current liabilities}}$$

Should the quick ratio be declining, the main problems are likely to relate to:

- production scheduling;
- stock control problems.

Debt to equity ratio (DER)

The debt to equity ratio is the percentage of total net assets that are made up of loans. High debt to equity ratios are a problem in most industries as cash flow must remain positive in order to pay the loans. Any figure above 60 per cent should cause considerable concern, especially in a period when interest rates can suddenly increase.

$$DER = \frac{\text{loans}}{\text{equity} + \text{loans}}$$

The only viable route that can be followed to improve the debt to equity ratio is either to raise more finance as equity or convert the loans to equity.

Interest cover

Interest cover is a measure of the times the positive cash flow of the company covers the interest payments due.

$$\text{Interest cover} = \frac{\text{loan interest}}{\text{net profit} + \text{loan interest}}$$

Interest cover of under 1.6 times is worrying.

Softawater, part V

The running review of the financial ratios reveals that the company is performing far better than in previous years (see Table 3.8).

Table 3.8   Softawater's financial ratio analysis

Items	Year to date	Previous year
Sales	8290	6320
Gross profit	5645	2740
Net profit	821	120
Stock and work in progress	1110	920
Fixed assets	510	420
Fixed costs	4992	2600
Administrative costs	1200	400
Sales and promotion costs	180	100
Debtors	830	650
Cash	180	20
Creditors	430	310
Tax	85	15
Borrowings	250	275
Equity	2155	1500
Loans	500	50
Bad debts	30	20
Interest paid	400	50
GPR	68	40
NP	10	2
ROCE	42	5
Breakeven value (£000)	7341	6046
Stock turn times/year	7.4	6.8
WCR	0.16	0.24
Debtor length (days)	36.5	37.5
Creditor length (days)	19	18
AER	14	11
SER	2	2
BDR	0.03	0.03
Current ratio	2.77	3.35
Quick ratio	1.32	1.1
DER	26	34
Interest cover	3.05	1.3

Sales are up, but profitability has grown at a higher rate than sales. Return on capital has jumped from an unacceptably low figure to one that the company is unlikely to be able to maintain next year, with the result that the working capital ratio has declined, showing that the company continues to use its assets more effectively. A worrying feature is that the breakeven value has risen considerably during the previous year. There has been a much higher administration bill than in previous years, and a consequence of this is the significantly higher interest payments on the investment the company has made to re-equip the factory.

Debtor length continues to be higher than the theoretical level of credit (30 days) given to customers. The problems of raw material supply for the industrial division continue to prove a problem for the creditor ratio, with the suppliers demanding payment against delivery for subcontracted work.

The current ratio remains high, as does the quick ratio. Interest cover has grown to a healthy position from a level that was barely sufficient. The debt to equity ratio has continued to improve, and the company has the facility to use the cash to further reduce the loan burden and enhance its profitability.

The main issue of concern in the financial ratio analysis is the growing level of administrative expense, which has been caused by higher salaries to the directors and more recruitment.

Benchmark

Softawater has significantly improved its financial position in the previous year. Most financial ratios are considerably ahead of those of its major competitors.

Brainstorm, part V

Brainstorm has continued to trade profitably and is now facing a major tax burden (see Table 3.9). With the high levels of cash held by the company, Brainstorm is in a position to undertake a whole range of strategic developments.

Table 3.9 Brainstorm's financial ratio analysis

Items	Year to date	Previous year
Sales	2350	2120
Gross profit	1645	1250
Net profit	555	410
Fixed assets	–	
Fixed costs	1090	1000
Administrative costs	360	300
Sales and promotion costs	35	30
Stock and work in progress	320	350
Debtors	35	38
Cash	750	550
Creditors	85	95
Borrowings	–	
Equity	780	680
Loans	–	–
Bad debts	–	–
Interest paid	–	–
GPR	70	59
NP	33	33
ROCE	71	60
Breakeven value (£000)	1557	1694
Stock turn times/year	7.3	6
WCR	43	39
Debtor length (days)	5.4	6.5
Creditor length (days)	13	16.3
AER	15	14
SER	1.4	1.4
BDR	–	–
Current ratio	11.6	9.8
Quick ratio	9.2	6.2
DER	–	–
Interest cover	–	–

Creditors continue to be paid more rapidly than would otherwise be the case as many of the suppliers offer 60 days' credit. It has been the policy of the company to pay bills on receipt and one of the directors continues to follow this initial plan.

Benchmark

A hardware retail company, Norton Hardware, is far more successful than Brainstorm in handling cash balances. By employing a firm of professional investment consultants, the company, although highly profitable in its own right, is generating approximately 50 per cent of its profits from investment rather than trading.

■ Production or service supply efficiencies

Production or service supply efficiencies measure the performance of the production or service supply system against agreed targets. They are relevant to taking future action, whether in the short or long term, to deal with problems mentioned here. See Chapter 4, for example.

Manufacturing or service efficiency ratio (MER)

The manufacturing or service supply efficiency ratio compares the actual variable cost with that which was originally planned. As a company produces more of a particular product, it should see a decline in the variable cost of production. This is known as the learning curve – the company is learning to produce a product more effectively. The overall effect of the learning curve varies from industry to industry and from product to product, but a rule of thumb is that every doubling of production volumes should mean a 6 per cent reduction in the overall cost.

$$MER = \frac{\text{actual costing}}{\text{standard costing}}$$

Declining MER ratios may be caused by:

- shorter runs with higher than expected start-up costs;
- longer production times per unit than expected;
- labour absenteeism;
- machinery problems;

- poor job costing;
- higher than expected raw material/labour costs.

Production or service productivity ratio (PPR)

This provides a measure of how effectively the production or service supply process is dealing with a particular level of volume compared with what was planned. It is a useful additional check on the manufacturing/service supply efficiency ratio discussed before in this section.

$$PPR = \frac{\text{actual sales/actual production hours}}{\text{planned sales/planned production hours}}$$

A poor PPR suggests:

- shorter production runs;
- poor production planning;
- machinery problems.

Material usage efficiency (MUR)

This measures how effectively the material and other bought in components are turned into products. This ratio is not applicable to all services, but would still be relevant to, say, a restaurant or transport service. It compares what should have been consumed in the standard production process with what should have been issued from stores based on a stock check.

$$MUR = \frac{\text{planned material issued from stores/planned sales}}{\text{actual material issued from stores/actual sales}}$$

The material usage ratio should operate within fairly narrow bands. Should the ratio be poor or declining, the following problems are likely to exist:

- theft;
- poor-quality components or raw materials;
- poor skills;
- machining problems;
- poor management control of production.

Start-up cost ratio (SUCR)

The start-up ratio analyses the amount of time machinery is in operation, compared with the total manufacturing time. Essentially, this is a measure that is useful to manufacturing rather than service businesses.

$$SUCR = \frac{\text{total manufacturing time}}{\text{total machine time}}$$

High start-up costs suggest one or more of the following:

- short production runs;
- poor machine flexibility;
- poor staff training;
- poor production planning.

Equipment utilisation ratio (EUR)

The equipment or machinery utilisation ratio provides a measure of the proportion of productive time used by equipment. The higher the level of equipment utilisation, the more productive the company is likely to be. The ideal situation would be to run equipment 24 hours a day, 365 days a year. Such a production plans means that the fixed costs of the operation are spread over as great a volume as possible, lowering the per unit cost of each product item or service produced (the economies of scale). Many services use equipment and this ratio is therefore valid for them.

$$EUR = \frac{\text{total time available/actual time}}{\text{total time available/planned time}}$$

A poor EUR ratio can be attributed to one or more of a number of factors:

- poor production planning;
- poor productivity;
- high levels of machine breakdown;
- poor order books.

 Maximise equipment utilisation to reduce fixed costs per unit.

Quality control ratio (QCR)

The quality control ratio is a measure of the number of complaints or product returns the company receives, compared with the planned level of problems. It is always weighted to take account of the volume of production or rate of service delivery.

$$QCR = \frac{\text{actual quality control problems/actual sales}}{\text{planned quality control problems/planned sales}}$$

A worsening quality control ratio needs rapid attention. The reason for the problem is likely to be self-evident, but will fall into one of the following three broad areas:

- staff failure;
- equipment failure;
- component failure.

A quality control ratio can also be used to define an acceptable level of raw material and component quality so that both the input and the output of the manufacturing process are measured. I shall return to the issue of product quality and complaints in 'Marketing efficiencies' later in this chapter, and when discussing product- or service-related improvements in Chapter 4.

CASE
STUDY

Softawater, part VI

Production still needs attention (Table 3.10). The production team has made significant strides in improving manufacturing productivity, although some of this has been due to the longer production runs. The job costing system requires significant overhauling as this appears to have been the main problem with the manufacturing efficiency ratio. There has not been a high level of theft – the material utilisation ratio again indicates a problem with the job costing system.

Both start-up costs and equipment utilisation ratios have improved as a result of the longer production runs, but there have been significant problems with quality control, which need immediate attention.

Table 3.10   Softawater's production efficiencies

Items	Actual year to date	Planned year to date
Sales (000s)	8290	8100
Cost per unit	0.38	0.35
Total stores issue (000s)	2487	2130
Total time available	8760	8760
Total machine time hours	2021	2000
Production hours	2367	2500
Total reject volume	55	25
Ratio analysis		
MER	92	
PPR	108	
MUR	87	
SUCR	106	
EUR	105	
QCR	200	

Benchmark

Aqua, one of Softawater's main competitors, has been working on a 24-hour production day. This initially enabled the company to achieve a certain amount of cost-cutting, but it is now facing the problem of having to replace a significant proportion of plant as the volume of rejects has increased.

■ Personnel efficiencies

A company is only as good as the people it employs. All companies should regularly review staff development and the extent to which the business is, or is not, creating problems for them. Remember that a business is not just an *economic* unit, it is the most crucial *social* component in many people's lives. When a company is very small, social issues can be dealt with on an informal basis, but this only works where numbers are quite small. Where there are more people, it is important to formalise the procedures for identifying and dealing with personnel problems – personnel efficiencies.

The evaluation of personnel efficiencies should be central to the planning and monitoring process once staff numbers exceed a level that can be controlled directly by senior management – say 30 or so. For the basic information system, it makes sense to organise all staff as full-time equivalents – that is, two individuals each working a half week are one full-time equivalent.

> *Remember that a business is not just an economic unit, it is the most crucial social component in many people's lives.*

Skills level

The level of skills was discussed in Chapter 2 as being one of the specific quantifiable objectives for the plan. The skills level is a key issue that must be continually reviewed and monitored as individuals join or leave the company or are trained internally or externally, because skills levels change and affect the achievement of the planned skills level within the company.

$$\text{Skills level} = \frac{\text{actual per capita skills level}}{\text{planned per capita skills level}}$$

A declining skills level is caused by one or more of the following:

- high turnover of skilled staff;
- a rapidly changing environment;
- poor training and recruitment.

Span of control

As companies grow in size, the need for supervisors increases, though the exact ratio of supervisors to workers will depend on the type of work carried out in the company and the level of skill of the staff. As a rule of thumb, a 12:1 ratio is generally the maximum – greater numbers result in a reduction in efficiency. This is generally the case, but each company has different requirements.

$$\text{Span of control} = \frac{\text{total staff}}{\text{supervisory management}}$$

The causes of a worsening span of control will be obvious – either a greatly increased number of staff or high turnover of supervisors.

Absenteeism

As stress increases, so, in general terms, does the level of absenteeism. The causes of this are similar to the causes of high staff turnover (see the next ratio), but it often provides early warning of the company losing staff.

$$\text{Absenteeism ratio} = \frac{\text{total number of days worked}}{\text{total number of available days}}$$

Staff turnover

The staff turnover ratio measures the effectiveness of the company in retaining staff. Every firm loses a proportion of its staff over time, but some are far better at keeping them than others. Keeping staff reduces training costs, generally improves the cohesiveness of the workforce (often called shared values), lowers recruitment costs and tends to increase workforce flexibility (though this statement needs to be treated with caution).

$$\text{Staff turnover} = \frac{\text{actual number of employees leaving}}{\text{planned turnover}}$$

High staff turnover is a symptom of:

- poor pay and other benefits;
- poor working conditions;
- poor work planning.

Disciplinary ratio (DR)

The disciplinary ratio measures how effectively rules and procedures are maintained within the company. It is important that all disciplinary issues are reported to a central review committee.

$$DR = \frac{\text{disciplinary}}{\text{total workforce}}$$

A worsening ratio may be caused by one of several factors:

- poor supervisory and upper-level management;
- increased levels of stress;
- poor documentation of formal rules;
- informal networks more important than formal ones.

Productivity

Employee productivity can be measured in two ways.

$$\text{Turnover per employee} = \frac{\text{total sales}}{\text{total number of full-time staff equivalents}}$$

$$\text{Profitability per employee} = \frac{\text{total profit}}{\text{total number of full-time staff equivalents}}$$

The reasons for declining ratios of productivity will again tend to be self-evident. Productivity is likely to be low as a result of:

- poor production planning;
- poor staff morale;
- absenteeism;
- poor order flow.

CASE STUDY

Softawater, part VII

Softawater has achieved a higher level of productivity per employee, both in terms of turnover and profitability, than was forecast in the plan. Skills levels have not been achieved as planned, although disciplinary records, staff turnover and absenteeism have been better than expected (Table 3.11 overleaf).

The company lost a number of its experienced supervisors during the year to competitors, and this has had a significant effect on the span of control, an issue that needs to be addressed quickly.

Benchmark

Aqua, the main consumer water purification competitor in the market, has proved more effective in managing its production base than Softawater over the past five years. It has trained and developed a much more skilled workforce and manages with a lower number of supervisory grade employees, yet continues to enjoy low levels of staff turnover and disciplinary problems.

Table 3.11   Softawater's personnel efficiencies

Items	Actual	Planned
Total sales (000s)	8290	8100
Total profit (000s)	821	700
Total employees	150	150
Total skills	2.6	2.8
Supervisory management	5	8
Total available days	38000	38000
Total days worked	37000	35000
Disciplinary actions	5	8
Leaving employees	8	20
Ratio analysis		
Skills ratio	92	
Span of control	30	18.75
Absenteeism	105	
Staff turnover	5	13
Disciplinary ratio	3	5
Productivity – turnover (000s)	55	54
Productivity – profit (000s)	5.5	4.6

CASE STUDY

Brainstorm, part VI

Brainstorm has highly positive ratios for all personnel elements. There has been low staff turnover, good skills development and high levels of productivity (Table 3.12).

Benchmark

Brainstorm has identified Cactus, a chain of franchised indoor plant retail outlets originally from the United States, as one of the key performers in raising productivity via a whole range of incentive schemes. These include stepped bonuses, competitions and personnel development, such as internal promotion schemes.

Table 3.12   Brainstorm's personnel efficiencies

Items	Actual	Planned
Total sales (000s)	2350	2100
Total profit (000s)	555	410
Total employees	24	26
Total skills	3.8	3.8
Supervisory management	4	4
Total available days	6072	6072
Total days worked	6005	5960
Disciplinary actions	–	–
Leaving employees	–	–
Ratio analysis		
Skills ratio	100	
Span of control	6	6
Absenteeism	101	
Staff turnover	–	–
Disciplinary ratio	–	–
Productivity – turnover (000s)	98	88
Productivity – profit (000s)	23	17

■ New product/service supply development efficiencies

Experience in new product or service development reveals that products/services reaching the market quickly, to specification and on budget, are more likely to be successful than those that fail to meet these criteria. These efficiencies are relevant to the discussion of short-term improvements in Chapter 4, and longer-term product development strategy in Chapter 6.

Number ratio

This is a straightforward comparison between the total number of new product introductions and what was forecast in the plan.

Time ratio

This ratio makes a straightforward comparison between the time taken to complete the new product development process and what was predicted in the plan – that is, the actual weeks of all projects combined compared with the planned weeks.

Budget ratio

The budget ratio simply compares the money spent on the new product development process with the amount planned. This reveals the level of efficiency, and the extent to which the budget has been overspent.

Specification achievement

Another straightforward assessment, this time of how closely the specification of new products has matched the planned performance criteria.

Commercial return

This makes a comparison between the planned and actual rates of return to the organisation, based on the chosen criteria of payback speed and net present value (see Chapter 8).

CASE
STUDY

Softawater, part VIII

The company has consistently failed to be effective in new product development. Over the past year, there have been fewer new products than were planned, and those that have been introduced have not achieved budget, time or specification criteria (Table 3.13).

Table 3.13 Softawater's new product development efficiencies

Items	Actual	Planned
Number	2	4
Time	60	100
Budget	50	100
Specification achievement	70	100
Commercial return	40	100

Benchmark

One of the main specialists in the supply of industrial water purification equipment in Germany, Wasser, has had a successful record over ten years of introducing leading-edge technology. The company has created a system of developing patented ideas in other industrial sectors into viable equipment for the water sector, via the use of dedicated new product development teams.

■ Marketing efficiencies

These efficiencies are relevant to much of the discussion on short-term action in Chapter 4, and long-term strategy in Chapters 5 and 6.

Quality standards

Every company establishes action standards for the delivery of a product or service. These might cover issues such as speed of service, completeness of knowledge for a service-based organisation or product and delivery quality for a manufacturing company. (A quality control ratio was given in the section on production efficiencies earlier in this chapter.)

Each SME has to establish its own action standards – however rough and ready these are initially – to regularly monitor the effectiveness of their service or product delivery. These action standards will, for example, consist of product weight, taste, colour, performance and reliability or, in the case of a service supplier, speed of service, cleanliness of outlet or expertise of assistance.

➡ **Maintaining quality standards is vital for any company. Good service and/or quality is mentioned to 3 colleagues or contacts, whereas bad service is mentioned to 20.**

Customer complaints

Customer complaints (also mentioned earlier as an element in the production efficiency ratios) are part of marketing quality management. They provide a measure of what is wrong with the organisation from an external perspective – and, after all, it is the customers who pay your salary.

A detailed examination of the volume of complaints, their exact nature and how they were handled should be a regular part of the monthly review.

Order book

For many companies in both the manufacturing and service sectors, a review of the forward order position is also an essential part of an information system.

Order size

Order size is another important part of the review for the marketing department. Every order has a fixed cost associated with it – the generation of paperwork, warehouse organisation, production set-up costs and so on. In a service environment, similarly, the service costs are incurred whether the order is small or large.

Monitoring the order level gives valuable information on whether or not the firm is achieving its sales targets and if a full range of products or services is being offered.

Order completeness

Split deliveries raise costs. It is in the interests of the company to be able to deliver complete or as near complete orders as possible in single deliveries or service supply. Where there are major problems in achieving this, the production, order processing or inventory system requires detailed attention.

Speed of delivery

The production and delivery cycle controls how quickly the company can generate cash and service the customer. It is in its interests to meet delivery targets – indeed, to improve on them if possible, subject to cost and customer requirements. Speed in the delivery of a service is no less important.

Discount level

The higher the discount level, the lower the level of profit. Monitoring discount levels against the plan will ensure that profitability targets are met, and that the price/volume relationship built into the plan is being maintained.

Logistical cost per unit

The efficiencies of the logistical system should be monitored to ensure that the target cost figures are being achieved.

Callage volume

Monitoring the total volume of sales calls provides an overview of the sales department's level of activity, though not, of course, of its effectiveness. Other review items that can be included in this sector are order volume per call, cost per call, total successes compared with total calls (see also Chapter 4, the section on sales fine-tuning and Table 4.4) .

Price per lead

The manufacturing and service SME should concentrate on generating sales leads from its promotional material.

Price per converted lead

The effectiveness of promotional material can be best measured by the leads that actually generate business.

CASE STUDY ## Softawater, part IX

The company has been achieving the majority of the targets set in its marketing plan. Action standards for product effectiveness are being achieved in the main, with the result that customer complaints are below the level expected. The order book is busier than anticipated due to the development of a new major outlet, which has had the effect of raising the average order size (Table 3.14).

With the larger order size, the company has been able to achieve a higher level of order completeness and has reduced the average time it takes to ship the order. Similar benefits have been seen in the level of discount and the logistical cost per unit.

Table 3.14   Softawater's marketing efficiencies

Items	Actual	Planned
Action standards	97	100
Customer complaints	15	25
Order book (000s)	2450	2300
Order size (000s)	1.2	0.8
Order completeness	97	95
Speed of delivering order (days)	10.8	12
Discount level %	3.5	5
Logistical cost per unit	11.8	12
Callage volume	1650	1800
Price per lead	50	67
Price per converted lead	400	350

Benchmark

Softawater is nearly as good as the most successful company in terms of customer service that it has been able to identify. This company, Balance, produces weighing machines for a whole range of consumer and industrial markets. It has established clearly defined action standards for company performance during the last ten years and monitors these continually, at shop floor level, at quality circles, supervisory, and senior management levels. With its sophisticated computer-based planning system and just in time (JIT) production based on sophisticated machine tools, orders are completely filled within five days. The high quality the company has achieved means that its discount rates are low, and careful monitoring of the distribution system continually achieves one of the lowest logistical unit costs in the industry.

SUMMARY

Information is central to the business planning exercise. This chapter has been about creating a company information system and techniques for the gathering of detailed information on the current state of an SME. We have seen how the collection of information for this purpose is a major initial step in preparing the detail for a business plan. Part of this exercise has involved decision making in a number of areas, including the appointment of the planning team.

Because the emphasis is on detail and there are variations in the information needs of each business, the approach chosen has been an exhaustive one. Some of the techniques described are therefore more relevant than others to particular businesses. An information system organised into eight main areas was suggested:

- cash flow;
- profit and loss statement;
- balance sheet;
- financial ratios;
- production/service supply efficiencies;
- new product/service supply development efficiencies;
- personnel efficiencies;
- marketing efficiencies.

By using the information gathered in these areas and applying the techniques described in the chapter to the case study companies – Softawater and Brainstorm – a clear and detailed analysis of the state of the two companies has been possible. We now know where they are currently, what they are doing well and where they are having problems. In this context, benchmarking is introduced, identifying what competitor companies do well or poorly.

Fine-tuning: work hard, work smart

1
2
3
4
5
6
7
8
9

INTRODUCTION

The fully developed information system, based on the detailed analysis of the previous year's performance, will be the foundation for managing the SME. The company's planner(s) must now look at how to use the information to improve current performance and competitive advantage without incurring substantial additional costs. This is the second part of using business planning to move forward (described at the beginning of Chapter 3).

This process of fine-tuning the existing business so that any new investment will achieve higher rates of return – because the underlying operation is being managed more effectively – is evaluated in this chapter. It is called fine-tuning here, but it is also essentially a consolidation strategy (Chapter 6).

In this chapter, I shall work back from the customer using a marketing approach. This contrasts with the last two chapters, which tended to move forward from finance. What I am doing here is emphasising the business plan as an integrated whole and so working back from the customer will make this clearer. You will see that different areas of the business contribute to the strength of the whole foundation, and that weakness in several of the blocks will affect the whole.

It is necessary to be clear about what can realistically be achieved in the short term and what requires higher levels of investment and is therefore part of the longer-term strategy discussed in the next chapter and forms part of the planning loop (see Figure 1.1, Chapter 1). What is achievable in the short term varies by company and industry. This chapter outlines improvements that are feasible for many SMEs in the short term. Each issue must be evaluated in the light of the peculiar circumstances of each company when deciding whether or not it should be included as part of the longer-term strategy to gain competitive advantage. There are certain broad conclusions that can be made about the likely timescale involved for changes in the various areas of the business and these are given in Table 4.1 – indicated by the amount of shading – showing the potential for achieving change over the short, medium or long term, the darkest being most difficult.

Table 4.1   The timescales required to achieve changes in specific areas of company activity

Area of activity	Short term	Medium term	Long term
Sales performance			
Promotional planning			
Product planning			
Logistical planning			
Production planning			
New product planning			
Facilities planning			
Administration planning			
Personnel planning			
Financial planning			

MANAGING FINE-TUNING

You will recall that the fine-tuning exercise began in Chapter 3 when various watch points and possible causes of problems were listed in the discussion of the various financial ratios and efficiencies. To get the best from this chapter, refer again to Chapter 3 and to the various efficiency ratios in particular. Assume you now have some or all of the following information gathered from the cash flow, profit and loss statement, various financial ratios, production efficiencies, marketing efficiencies and so on. How can you use this information to make improvements in:

- sales call performance;
- promotional planning;
- product or service planning;
- distribution/logistical planning;
- production planning;
- new product/service development planning;
- facilities planning;
- administration planning;
- personnel planning;
- financial planning?

83

Table 4.1 shows that certain planning areas are more suitable for the fine-tuning exercise than others.

As with the information system exercise, a team should be formed on a similar basis (Chapter 3). It can consist of those responsible for the development of the information system. What the SME wants from this team is a report on how to make improvements in the current business operation. The crucial issue is to ensure that the quality of customer service is not adversely affected.

■ Responsibility, timescales and reporting format

Individual staff will investigate particular areas of the company operation and report back on the improvements that can be achieved by implementing some or all of the suggestions outlined in the following sections. Each staff member should complete a reporting sheet, which can be designed to suit each particular company requirement (Table 4.2).

Table 4.2 Fine-tuning the reporting format for sales

Items	Responsibility	Can implement?	Action
Sales independents			
Wholesalers			

FINE-TUNING SALES

■ Company sales force versus independents

If sales force costs are rising out of control, the options of subcontracting part of the sales activity or concentrating sales force coverage on the more profitable activities alone should be considered as part of the plan.

The use of independents has disadvantages, in lack of control, training, and promotional activity, but it can be useful for minor accounts or areas that are difficult to service. Wholesalers can also be considered to service particular accounts or areas. Many companies establish a minimum order quantity for them to service directly, while wholesalers service orders below that minimum.

■ Journey planning

Is the cost of sales representatives' time a major expense? Studies indicate that introducing journey planning can lower the costs per call by up to 60 per cent. A further improvement that can be made to journey planning is to categorise customers so that they receive a clear and appropriate level of service. It is sensible, therefore, to categorise the callage rate according to the volume of business, and review this on a regular basis. You can set out the information in table form along the lines of Table 4.3.

Table 4.3   Example of a table that can be used to categorise callage rates to improve journey planning

Category	Sales volumes	Callage rate
A	More than x	Fortnightly
B	Between y and z	Monthly
C	Less than z	Three times a year

■ Improving the effectiveness of each call

By the time a lighted match has burnt down to the fingers a sales call will have succeeded or failed. This illustrates the time constraints on a sales call. Developing an approach that improves the chances of gaining the attention of buyers is likely to pay

> *By the time a lighted match has burnt down to the fingers a sales call will have succeeded or failed.*

substantial dividends. The main elements are:

- understanding buyers' problems – most buyers want solutions not just products;
- a written agenda – this will take the buyer quickly through the various issues and can be left behind as a reminder of the visit;
- simple demonstration material;
- complementary sales.

Planning can improve the potential of each sales call by considering the potential other avenues, which can be explored during the meeting. Thus, a secondary objective would be to offer products or services that are complementary to the core product (the primary objective), while gathering information that could improve the possibility of additional sales would be a tertiary objective. Low-cost training and monitoring of sales staff in the development of sales objectives often yields valuable returns.

■ Improving the performance of individual sales representatives

The performance of sales representatives (mentioned in the discussion of marketing efficiencies and activity ratios in Chapter 3) is crucial to the SME's success. Individual sales representatives can be compared with their colleagues using key performance indicators, as shown in Table 4.4, together with an example. Sales representative B, while covering a lower percentage of the total customer base and having only a slightly higher success rate, is far more productive than sales representative A. This should lead sales management to review the reasons behind the different levels of achievement of the two representatives.

Table 4.4   Sales representative productivity

Factor	Representative A	Representative B
Total number of potential customers	500	500
Total number contacted	400	300
% market coverage	80	60
Total number of calls	1200	1000
Average calls per customer	3	3.3
Total number of sales	650	600
Total value of sales	150,000	250,000
% success rate	54	60
Total cost incurred by sales representative	35,000	30,000
Cost per sale	54	50
Return (total value of sales/total cost)	4.3	8.3

■ Communications

As the cost of selling time increases, improved communication between the sales representative and head office generates additional business. It also benefits the company as it speeds up order processing.

■ Pricing and marginal profitability

The revenue stream is highly dependent on the prices that can be obtained in the market. It is important for any business to reduce the level of discount offered. Useful techniques to reduce or control discounting are to:

- alter delivery quantities (though this may have cost implications and you need to be certain of the effect this will have on customer service);
- use certain sales promotion techniques – for example, banding or bundling other items with the sales package, and buyer incentives, such as paying for certain promotion material (this will have cost implications but these are nearly always lower than a discount, which applies across the entire order);
- quote special prices for large contracts.

  In the last case, when the firm has the possibility of gaining a significant volume of business from a large contract, a special pricing formula – marginal profitability or marginal pricing – will significantly increase the potential of gaining the business. The important issue is that the large contract is additional business to the company over and above existing volumes.

The existing information system will show the current level of gross profit and fixed costs (both mentioned in Chapter 3). An example of this is given in Table 4.5, which shows that the existing business generates a gross margin of 30 per cent and a net margin of 15 per cent, indicating that all the fixed costs are adequately absorbed by the existing business and that any additional volume can be competitively priced as these costs are already absorbed.

Table 4.5   Analysing cost recovery in the existing business

Revenue/cost centre	Sales	Income (cost)
Standard business	1000	300
Fixed costs		(150)
Profit		150

As the level of discount from the normal price increases, the chances of gaining the additional business are also enhanced. Experience will suggest the potential relationship between the level of discount and the chances of winning the business – often called a competitive bidding model. As the price falls, so will the gross margin. Multiplying together a price index based on current market pricing (average standard pricing = 100), the gross margin at that price level, and the percentage chance of winning the contract at that price provides an overall measure of the potential return to the business. In the example shown in Table 4.6, the highest level of return will be achieved by a 10 per cent discount on the standard price (90 x 17 x 0.5 = 765).

Table 4.6   Example of a competitive bidding model

Price index	Margin %	Chances of winning contract	Returns
100	30	0.1	300
90	17	0.5	765
80	5	0.9	360

There are two vital factors that must be taken into account when such a marginal profitability or competitive bidding system is introduced:

- the business needs to be completely certain of its costing environment – that it has accurately separated variable costs from fixed costs, and that there will be no nasty surprises;
- gaining the contract will not cause any major financing problems.

Adding the value of the contracted business to the existing cash flow will enable the business planner to check the viability of the proposed contract before it is signed.

■ Major customer contract

Production planning, physical distribution planning, inventory planning, sales call planning, promotion planning, cash flow planning are all simplified if the company can enter into a contract with major customers. The greater the percentage of business that can be stabilised in this fashion, the more effective the organisation can become. There is often, of course, a trade-off to consider – lower margins in return for guaranteed production, as the customer demands planned promotions, and guaranteed levels of discount. The main components of a trade marketing agreement are listed in Table 4.7.

Table 4.7   Trade marketing agreement

Volume	Logistics	Promotion	Price
Monthly off-take Minimum stock levels Size of delivery Mixed stock order	Planned delivery Emergency delivery Returns	Promotional allowances Sales training Space allocation Media planning Sales visits Special packs	Quantity discounts Free goods Credit

■ Credit terms

The ideal, in terms of cash flow, is for customers to pay cash – any credit term will cause problems. The longer the credit terms, the greater the problem. Managing credit at customer level is a far better solution than attempting to control it via the credit control system. Strict control over the terms to the customer and attempting to reduce the credit length should be part of the sales programme, with the aim to steadily reduce the company's average credit length.

■ Travel expenses

Remember that part of the exercise is to keep customers happy and so attacking this cost burden is not an entirely simple issue – lower costs do not necessarily mean better performance. Various approaches can be considered, all of which have benefits in that they reduce costs while maintaining the quality of sales provision:

- limiting the entire company to fuel-efficient cars;
- using discount organisations when booking travel and hotels;
- limiting per diem expenditure to a certain target figure, providing that actual expenditure is always supported by receipts.

■ Motivation

Making sure that the sales force is properly motivated yields immediate benefits. Studies show that money is not the sole motivating factor and, indeed, becomes less important the longer an individual remains with a company. Motivational components include:

- physical environment;
- job content;
- responsibility;
- job prospects;
- training;
- group recognition;
- job title;
- fringe benefits;
- compensation.

For many, low-cost investment in a particular motivational mix may produce a high level of return.

■ Pay structure

Pay that is received regardless of performance is a major burden for many companies, especially with, say, a highly paid team such as the sales force. It is in the company's interest to move away from a fixed pay structure to one that comprises fixed and performance-related components. Bonus schemes, if they are introduced, should meet a number of criteria. They should be:

- transparent;
- equitable;
- responsive to individual performance;
- achievable.

■ New technology in sales management

A host of sales management software packages exist to give support to the SME without costing the earth, unless you buy all of them, of course! For example, there are packages to aid the development of journey planning, managing and developing customer accounts, analysing the performance of sales representatives and developing effective motivational campaigns.

CASE STUDY

Softawater, part X

Softawater could carry out a number of the suggested improvements in the organisation of its sales operations. The use of independents is not considered relevant to the current operation, but dealing with smaller customers via wholesalers would significantly improve the profitability of the operation. On closer examination of the performance of its sales representatives there appear to be wide differences between the achievements of individual sales representatives. A detailed investigation of the reasons for these differences has led to a significant improvement in overall performance.

The company currently does not have a sophisticated journey planning system in place and the introduction of such a system would improve efficiency. A demonstration system might improve sales, as would the development of more effective sales literature. An attempt at developing complementary sales has not yet taken place, but it could yield benefits.

Communications could be significantly improved at low cost. Present pricing and credit terms allow little freedom for manoeuvre. Softawater does not have large contract work to tender for – market-led pricing dominates the sector and credit terms are universal for all of the suppliers. However, it has held initial discussions with some major customers to explore the possibility of signing a trade marketing agreement. The response has been positive and the company is putting together a proposal for negotiation.

Travel expenditure has been rising for the last three years, without adequate control. Bulk buying and the use of hotel chain discount systems are obvious methods of improving efficiency in this area. Restructuring sales representatives' pay and improving the motivational 'mix' could also mean improved performance at a lower cost.

PROMOTION-RELATED IMPROVEMENTS

■ Channels

Has the company chosen the most cost-effective promotional channel for its investment? Big companies' promotional expenditure is based on high-cost downwards planning, but the SME's emphasis should be on low-cost upwards planning. In other words, SMEs should be concentrating on the least costly option that is effective. This policy should focus SMEs' expenditure in areas that can provide measurable, action-oriented response, rather than simply create 'awareness'.

For the SME, a combination of sales representatives and sales promotion is likely to provide the most cost-effective combination, although there are certain media channels that are well worth considering as experience suggests that they are also a very cost-effective means of generating sales. All the following channels are capable of including specific response material that requires the customer to act – leading to either a sale or the generation of a sales lead:

- directories;
- local press;
- direct mail;
- exhibitions;
- low-cost public relations via a newsletter or press release activity;
- telephone canvassing;
- the Internet.

Different methods of commonly used sales promotion techniques in various consumer and industrial sectors are in Table 4.8.

Table 4.8   Sales promotion options for the SME

Options	Advantages	Disadvantages	Timescale	Appropriateness of method
Buyer incentive	Trial, repeat purchase, targeted	Cost, contrary to company rules	Short	Yes, but with care
Competition	Improve image, repeat purchase, targeted, can build database	Design and control	Medium and long	Difficult
Lottery	Repeat purchase	Image and control	Medium and long	Difficult
Added value pack	Repeat purchase, channel loyalty	Cost, effect on pricing, production	Short and medium	Only with sophisticated production
Banded pack	Repeat purchase, targeted	Production cost	Short	Yes
Sales accelerator	Better display, targeted	High cost, maintenance	Medium and long	Difficult
Self-liquidating offer	Repeat purchase, can build database	Image and control, production cost	Medium and long	Difficult
Coupon	Trial, repeat purchase	Difficult logistics, image	Medium and long	Yes, with care
Merchandising, special event, point-of-sale	Repeat purchase, image	Cost and coverage, logistics	Medium and long	Yes, with care
Sample	Trial, targeted	Production, cost, logistics	Medium and long	Yes, with care
Bar code	Repeat purchase, targeted	Cost	Short	Yes
Discount	Repeat purchase	Cost, pricing implications	Short	Yes, with care
Credit	Repeat purchase	Cost, cash flow	Short to medium	Difficult
Loyalty reward	Repeat purchase, complementary sale, database	Control, service support	Medium to long	Yes, with care

Table 4.9 Advantages and disadvantages of the various media channels for the SME

Channels	Advantages	Disadvantages	Planning horizon	Can SME use?
Television	Coverage, build-up, colour, movement	High cost, control, information content limited, measurement difficult	Medium to long	Possible, low-cost, local TV
Radio	Coverage, build-up, cost	Information content, no colour or movement, target audience	Short to medium	Local radio can be effective
Cinema	Good colour, movement	Cost, customer profile evaluation	Medium to long	Can be used as local poster equivalent
Magazines	Visual, target customers, response material	Slow build-up, cost	Medium	Specialist, market access
National press	Visual, build up, response material	Image, cost, colour, evaluation	Short to medium	Limited use
Regional press	Visual, build up, response material, cost, evaluation	Coverage	Short	Useful for many SMEs
Directories	Cost, target audience	Readership	Medium to long	Useful support
Poster	Local focus, long time period, colour	Information content, impact, evaluation	Medium to long	Doubtful
Exhibitions	Target audience, full product demonstration	Cost, manpower, space, success of organisers crucial	Long	Where returns are certain
Direct mail	Target audience, response material, information, cost per lead	Design crucial, mailing list crucial, follow-up important	Short to medium	Can be very effective
Telephone contact	Target audience, cost per lead	Customer response, image problems, information content	Short	Design, control vital
Internet	Cost per lead, information, content, international	Follow-up problems, additional promotion necessary, design update, targeting difficult	Short to medium	For certain service companies
Public relations	Low cost if good content, coverage, information	High cost if content poor, control difficult, evaluation impossible	Short to medium	Local PR can work well
Sponsorship	Raises awareness	Cost, target audience, association with problem events, evaluation	Long term	Limited use

There are 14 main media methods of reaching the consumer, each of which has its own particular strengths and weaknesses (Table 4.9).

For the SME, the objective must be to find a method of promotion that works by generating trial and repeat sales. This means that the company has to experiment with all the available techniques in order to find those that are most suited to its needs. Benchmarking is particularly useful in this area, seeing what other companies do and how effective it is.

■ Seasonality

It is important to realise that all sales generated by advertising are linked to the sales level at a particular time. Companies with significant seasonality of sales will find that expenditure on promotion is more cost-effective at times of peak sales than during fallow periods. Spending the promotional budget during these peak sales times will produce higher levels of return from the same budget.

■ Frequency of expenditure

Research shows that, for the majority of products (except those with a complicated sales message and/or strongly seasonal sales), continuous promotion is far more effective than concentrating expenditure into short periods of time (see above). Here again the company can generate a greater sales level from the same budget by restructuring when the budget is available.

■ The message

For the SME, a simple message will produce better returns than a highly sophisticated one. Planners should concentrate on messages that say:

- who you are;
- what you do;
- why customers should buy what you are selling;
- how they can buy it.

Including a method of response generally produces a higher level of return than if it is not included. Such response methods include:

- coupons;
- reply-paid cards;
- Freefone telephone number.

■ In-house material creation

A considerable proportion of the cost of literature and other promotional material lies in their origination. Developing expertise in using low-cost software means that designs for promotional material can be rapidly and cheaply evaluated and produced to print standards.

■ Government or trade association support

Government or local trade associations can often be a source of support for marketing initiatives, either by providing information on potential customers or subsidising promotional investment.

■ Pricing/promotional optimisation

Heavily advertised, market-leading products can be sold for a higher price than the less well-advertised, but similar quality, competition. Where companies have increased their media promotion as part of their plan, pricing could possibly be increased without a substantial loss of business.

CASE STUDY | Brainstorm, part VII

Brainstorm is far from optimising its promotional planning. It has not fully exploited the available promotional channels, especially public relations activity. Indeed, its planning for seasonal sales is haphazard and most of the expenditure has been made later than it should be.

The company has an amateur approach to the development of promotional materials and frequency of expenditure and does not exploit possible links with the trade organisation, which could help in some areas of expenditure.

With its low level of promotional spend there are few opportunities to raise the prices of its products.

PRODUCT- OR SERVICE-RELATED IMPROVEMENTS

New product or service development efficiencies form part of the data collected for the information system presented in Chapter 3. Remember that here we are concerned with the short term, but much of product or service development is longer term so this is covered in Chapter 6.

■ Understanding customer requirements

Basic and simple market research can do much to improve competitive advantage by serving the customer better. A detailed insight into the company's position in the market can be obtained from regular, straightforward, telephone or written questionnaires with a few questions.

- Do you get good service?
- Is the product range wide enough to supply all your requirements?
- Are there internal issues that prevent the company from providing the best service/product?
- How can we improve our product or service?

For many companies it will make sense to standardise such reviews as part of the information system and include them as part of the analysis of customer complaints (Chapter 3 – Production or service supply efficiencies and Marketing efficiencies).

■ Improving quality

Poor-quality raw materials, component supplies, and finished goods or services raise costs and interrupt production. Setting clearly defined raw material and component supply specifications and closely monitoring each supply batch by random sampling will do much to improve the quality of the components and reduce production hiccups. Setting similar standards for the finished product will further broaden the impact of quality on the position of the market.

Quality improvements have a variety of short- and long-term effects, which can be summarised (Table 4.10).

Table 4.10   The effects of quality on short- and long-term company performance

Factor	Initial results	Long-term results
Improved performance	Improved reputation, higher prices	Greater market share, greater volume, improved economies of scale
Reduced component failure	Increased productivity, lower rework and scrap, lower guarantee costs	Lower production costs, lower service costs
Increased staff commitment	Higher productivity	Lower staff turnover, higher skills

■ Supplier contracts

Creating long-term contracts with suppliers often has significant value in terms of improving quality, achieving delivery and price targets and smoothing cash flow. These contracts allow the firm to build long-term relationships with its suppliers – a crucial factor in many manufacturing and service companies. Even in the short term, these contracts can focus both the supplier and the company on the central quality control and service issues that need to be developed for the long term.

DISTRIBUTION/LOGISTICAL IMPROVEMENTS

Logistical improvements are most likely to be relevant in a manufacturing environment. With the wide scope of the service sector, there will be issues that inevitably apply to some or all service companies – order processing and technology for example.

■ Third-party distribution

Subcontracting all or part of the distribution function has proved very successful for many companies. Running and maintaining lorries and warehouses is not an area of expertise among most service or manufacturing companies, and considerable cost savings can be achieved by an evaluation of the potential for change.

■ Shared transport

Where third-party distribution is not possible, shared transport, especially for long-distance deliveries, may be an option. Many SMEs fail to explore the possibilities of establishing links with other local companies facing similar distribution dilemmas, especially those that are not direct competitors.

■ Change in physical distribution method

As customers and products change, and costs of transport, the chosen physical distribution system may not remain the most cost-effective one. Faster distribution means lower storage or inventory costs. However, it may also mean higher ordering costs and higher transport costs. For most companies, the choice is limited to one or two alternatives, but it is worth, from time to time, looking at other methods as part of the planning exercise. For example, air freight, for many companies, is becoming a viable option, but one that is not often evaluated. There is an equation that integrates the components that need to be assessed for each transport type:

$$\text{cost crossover} = \text{transport cost} + \text{inventory or storage cost} + \text{customer's inventory cost} + \text{ordering cost}$$

which, in full, is:

$$C = rD + utD + a/s + wsD/2 + wk (s + t+k)D1/2$$

where: $C = \text{cost}$
$D = \text{total annual demand}$
$r = \text{transport cost}$
$t = \text{average delivery time}$
$s = \text{average time between shipments}$
$u = \text{inventory or storage cost}$

w = inventory storage cost at customer premises

a = set-up costs of production

k = cost of stock.

■ Improved physical distribution planning

The introduction of a journey planning system for physical distribution, similar to that for the sales representative, can also improve efficiency at little cost. There are manual systems that provide a considerable degree of sophistication for improved control, though computer programmes can give a very high level of control for limited expenditure.

■ Order processing

Approximately 2 per cent of the total cost is accounted for by the order processing system. Improvements to this system can:

- speed production, reducing working capital and improving the return on capital employed;
- improve the internal controls to ensure that orders, and documentation, are effectively completed on time;
- improve effectiveness of production management by phasing orders according to defined criteria;
- provide a more effective customer service by providing more and reliable information on order completion and delivery dates.

■ Warehousing

The storage costs of inventory and the way in which it is stored can also be tackled by means of a re-evaluation of the warehousing system. Important issues are whether or not:

- the company should be using leased or owned facilities or renting third-party space;
- more efficient handling methods in the existing warehousing system would speed order delivery and reduce costs;
- warehouse layout could be reorganised so that the most frequently ordered products are kept closely together to speed order collection and despatch;

- the layout of the warehouse could be improved so that a smaller area is used for storage, enabling the company to continue to grow without needing new space.

■ Inventory levels

Maintaining stock is a major area of cost that should be minimised wherever possible. There are several options that you can investigate if you are looking for ways of reducing the overall stock-holding.

- **Raw material/component supply**   Will the supplier hold stock against which orders can be placed when required? Can smaller quantities of raw materials/components be ordered on a frequent and regular basis to replace larger, single orders?
- **Back order potential**   Can orders be supplied only when the order has been placed by the customer (known as back ordering)? Will the customer be prepared to wait the necessary time? Can we speed the production process to meet the delivery schedule?

■ Safety stock

Companies hold safety stock in case of variations in the order flow from customers. The level of safety stock is a management decision based on how frequently the company is prepared to be out of stock when customers place orders. Often, it is a blanket decision applying to all products. The reality is that, for most companies, there are considerable differences between products, and this would enable them to create separate categories for products, permitting lower safety stock levels for some.

Many companies will see three main categories of products which are shown in Table 4.11 (overleaf).

Table 4.11 Categories of products and how acceptable it is for them to be out of stock

Category	Type of product	Acceptable percentage of times out of stock
A	Major profit-earner	5%
A	New product introduction	5%
A	Crucial spare part	5%
B	Medium profit-earner	15–20%
B	Minor spare part	15–20%
C	Minor profit-earner	25–30%

A final element in analysing safety stock is how stock is held within a network of warehouses. As the number of sites increases, the level of safety stock also grows. Reducing the number of sites at which certain stocks are held has a considerable effect on the overall stock-holding, although this, of course, has implications in other areas of the business – physical distribution, order processing and warehouse management, for example.

■ Reorder level

The reorder level depends on the level of safety stock and the speed at which the production system can manufacture the stock. Changing how production manages its orders can further reduce stockholdings by shortening the time period necessary to manufacture.

■ Economic order quantity (EOQ)

The economic order quantity equation enables you to make an assessment of the quantity of products that should be produced at any one time.

$$EOQ = \sqrt{2 \, (DS) / IC}$$

where: EOQ = economic order quantity
D = annual demand
S = set-up cost of the particular product
I = annual stockholding cost as a percentage of total cost
C = price per unit

Companies can reduce the economic order quantity in a number of ways. The most effective is to spend time analysing the level of set-up costs and try to reduce these. Another approach is to reduce the overall level of stockholding pertaining to a particular product. Relevant here is the earlier discussion, in this section, of approaches to setting the level of safety stock.

■ New technology in logistics

Computer software exists to manage the entire logistical function more effectively. For example, it can be used to define types and frequency of physical distribution, help with the warehouse function, speed order processing and completeness of despatch.

CASE STUDY Softawater, part XI

Product quality could be improved with the introduction of more rigorous quality control checks to further reduce the level of customer complaints. Softawater already carries out regular market questionnaires with its major customers.

A detailed analysis of Softawater's logistics suggests that there are several improvements that could be made to the current operation. The company already uses third-party distribution, and cannot take advantage of shared transport. There are no advantages to be had in changing the type of physical distribution system employed nor, with a third party-distribution system, would improved load planning be possible. However, the company can make the order processing system speedier by standardising order forms and improving internal communications within the factory. It can also make major reductions in inventory levels by introducing back ordering for certain customers, thus lowering the level of safety stock and improving the economic order quantity by reducing the start-up costs of the production process.

PRODUCTION PLANNING IMPROVEMENTS

Techniques for working out production or service supply efficiencies were discussed as part of the information control system in Chapter 3. Many of the issues discussed will also have relevance to some or all service companies.

■ Subcontract

Subcontractors can reduce costs in certain areas of production by removing the need for expensive machines, smoothing fluctuations in the manufacturing flow by reducing peak loads, and bringing valuable outside expertise to the production of certain components and processes.

■ Personnel structure

When staff positions change due to retirement, resignation or promotion, it is always sensible to re-evaluate the position now vacant. Has the job changed? Can it be done by other members of staff?

Provided that key skills are not lost and support for the customer remains intact, reducing the numbers employed will obviously have a major impact on profitability. The company skills structure formed part of the setting of quantifiable specific objectives described in Chapter 2; and personnel efficiencies were also a part of the planning information system set out in Chapter 3.

▷ **Downsizing is dangerous unless the company retains the old potential in the new form.**

■ Pay structure

If the SME organises pay overall in the same way that was described earlier with regard to the sales force – away from fixed pay and towards a fixed plus variable/performance-related system – it will have benefits.

■ Production or service supply layout

Better production layouts, to improve the flow of goods through the manufacturing process, also creates an improved working atmosphere and helps reduce any potential health and safety problems. Various other possibly relevant aspects of layout have been discussed in Warehousing earlier in this chapter.

■ Production planning

Production planning improvements:

- reduce the amount of money tied up in work in progress;
- decrease the amount of space taken up by finished stock and work in progress;
- speed up production;
- improve the working environment by smoothing the workload;
- make employees aware of all the work needing to be completed and of the order in which it should be done.

■ Planned maintenance

Broken-down machinery and lack of spare parts is a common contributor to lower levels of productivity and lengthened production cycles in an SME. Planned maintenance reduces the chances of breakdown during peak production periods – as components are replaced at fixed intervals before they fail.

■ Internal quality control

Maintaining quality control, either during manufacturing or at the final stage, is an often significant cost for the average SME. Internal quality control checks – including making individual employees responsible for what enters and leaves their area of production or service provision – helps improve quality and reduce the cost of the operation. The introduction of such systems is vital in the initial development of certification processes such as ISO 9000 or ISO 14000.

■ Production or service staff support

Surveys indicate that a substantial proportion of production or service supply time is spent in a non-productive fashion in activities such as drinking, eating and travelling. Improving the support that the company provides workers in these areas – vending machines, for example, for coffee supply – can increase the level of productive work without involving major cost.

■ Employees' suggestions

Studies show that a well-run employee suggestion scheme yields the highest return of any activity within the company. A quality circle – building quality into the product service – is easy for most firms to introduce. It merely involves the discussion of the current week's production – problems and successes, and the forthcoming week's work – improvements that can be introduced, support from other areas of the company that could improve the job performance and training that is required.

■ Other help with production/service supply planning improvements

Production management software systems help managers to plan production more effectively. For example, they can be used to control stocks and identify problems with machinery utilisation and availability.

CASE STUDY | ## Softawater, part XII

A review of Softawater's production process reveals areas that can be improved without requiring significant investment. Management now takes the view that it has subcontracted too much of its production in the industrial sector and cannot subcontract more in the consumer products division. However, the company could make major improvements in quality control by monitoring its raw materials and components more carefully, improving internal quality control checks and developing quality circles, as well as encouraging its employee suggestion scheme.

Production planning could also be improved, with certain changes to layout and the introduction of a system of planned maintenance. Changes to personnel structure would be unlikely to yield major improvements as the company already has a thin structure. Alterations to the compensation system would require more detailed thought, though the introduction of a bonus system would appear to be the direction in which the company should move. The company could improve its industrial pricing with the completion of ISO 9000, and complete ISO 14000 for German and French industrial customers.

NEW PRODUCT OR SERVICE DEVELOPMENT IMPROVEMENTS

New product development efficiencies form part of the planning information system in Chapter 3. Product or service development is a long-term process and there are few changes that can be introduced immediately to significant effect. Improving the information flow to the project and clarifying reporting structures and authority, however, can have an immediate impact, but the majority of the key elements of successful product development are longer term (see Chapter 6).

CASE STUDY

Softawater, part XIII

Softawater continues to fail with its new product development, but it nevertheless remains a major area of expenditure. There are improvements that can be made in all areas of management – structure, the effective integration of new product development activity, project management, team creation, idea collection, protocol development and commercialisation. The only short-term improvements that could be achieved would be to widen the information collection system and clarify the job descriptions of the team members and their reporting structure.

FACILITIES IMPROVEMENTS

■ Rent and rates

Any reduction in the burden of these overheads can substantially improve profitability for most SMEs. Firms need to invest, where necessary, in professional advice to reduce potential rent increases, and lobby local administrations for property tax rebates or equivalent.

■ Utilities

The expenditure on utilities can be reduced in a number of ways:

- altering the supplier without damaging quality of supply;
- schedule some activities – particularly the more expensive – for off-peak periods, if special rates are available;

- improved control systems – for example, offices can have heating and lighting individually controlled with personnel-sensitive sensors, while warehouses can improve their heating by means of simple fans and air circulation systems;
- improved equipment efficiency – servicing or maintaining equipment at a higher level is also likely to have the impact of reducing utility cost.

CASE STUDY

Brainstorm, part VIII

Brainstorm does not have an effective policy for negotiating at the end of each rental period, so the involvement of a professional negotiator would probably yield significant benefits, in terms of both property rent and property taxes. Neither has it investigated any of the areas of utility control. It still uses the national telephone system, as well as existing water and electricity suppliers. It has made no attempt to introduce effective thermostats into its retail outlets, or power-saving systems into its tills and computers.

ADMINISTRATION IMPROVEMENTS

■ Subcontract

Similar advantages to subcontracting in production, logistics and sales may exist for administration.

■ External information sourcing

Companies will often be able to take advantage of the free or relatively cheap information available in trade associations, trade magazines, databases and official information sources.

■ Meetings, technology and planning

Fixed agendas, limited timescales and clear objectives can do much to improve each meeting's productivity. Technology improvements now enable companies to communicate far more effectively, whether internally or outside. Video conferencing, for example, can significantly reduce both the time and money spent at expensive meetings (especially if you include the costs of travel) – telephone conferencing methods are another example.

Making use of technological improvements in internal communications – including e-mail and voice mail – reduces the amount of paper required and speeds effective communications between key members of staff. The development of bulletin boards, either maintained physically or electronically, will help groups work together more effectively.

■ Improving internal data collection and organisation

Technology has substantially improved the effectiveness of the data collection and processing systems in a number of ways:

- the speed with which information is delivered;
- the quality of the information (provided that the system has been properly designed);
- it has become quicker to both input and analyse data.

For the SME, these improvements can be maximised by means of direct management input rather than the use of other administrative staff because they facilitate the following improvements to be made to procedures without incurring huge costs:

- standardised documentation;
- accounting software packages significantly improve the control those managing the financial side of things have over day-to-day financial management as they identify cash flow problems and highlight debtor and creditor issues that need to be clarified;
- creating the appropriate invoicing and paperwork for deliveries.

■ Professional support

You should carefully review the costs of professional support (your accountant, lawyer, consultant) to separate those services that are essential from those which could either be totally removed or significantly reduced by making changes in company procedures and installing appropriate systems.

Softawater, part XIV

....

There are a few areas in which Softawater can improve on its current operation. It has already minimised the costs of professional support by maintaining an accurate, computerised accounting system, but project management software would potentially improve the control the company has over projects. The company already uses job costing and production planning systems.

The number of administrative staff is relatively low in comparison with other firms and there are few opportunities for subcontracting. Internal communications are a problem and a number of initiatives could be developed to help in this area. Information sourcing has been amateurish, and developing links with the local trade association would significantly improve understanding of the market without incurring large costs.

....

PERSONNEL IMPROVEMENTS

We looked at staffing earlier in the production or service improvements section of this chapter and noted the fact that personnel skills form part of the specific quantifiable objectives listed in Chapter 2; and that personnel efficiencies are a part

> *Company culture must be supportive of the plan because it is people who make the plan work.*

of the planning information system described in Chapter 3. The point that needs to be made here is that company culture must be supportive of the plan because it is people who make the plan work.

An SME's culture is complicated. It depends on the:

- type of work or area of activity;
- company's physical environment;
- authority and responsibility structure;
- formal and informal procedures within the company;
- company's corporate image;
- recruitment policy;
- the communication systems, both formal and informal;
- and a number of other factors.

The most effective organisation has a culture that supports the overall objectives of the plan. Where conflict is developing between the culture and the plan, changes to the culture will need to be considered. Many of the necessary changes can only be carried out over the long-term, but some of the issues can be dealt with in the short term (Table 4.12).

Table 4.12 Personnel components and the potential for change in the short term

Issues	Components	Function	Short-term change
Structure	Job description, authority, responsibility, reporting systems, reporting frequency	Directs, controls, integrates	Job description, group working structure
Staff	Number of staff, staff demographics		Change numbers
Skills	Task skills, knowledge	Builds competitive advantage	Building key skills
Systems	Recruitment, appraisal, training, discipline, information, motivation	Integrates, builds shared values, increases productivity, lowers staff turnover	Widen and clarify recruitment policy, strengthen flow of information, increase appraisal, increase counselling, simple bonus scheme, open promotion
Support	Work planning, technology, working area, work conditions	Increases productivity, builds competitive advantage	Improve work scheduling, improve work area, improve conditions
Shared values	Common attitudes, common goals	Commitment, flexibility	
Style	Authoritarian, bureaucratic, democratic	Implements, integrates, builds shared values	

■ Cost

Cutting the cost of personnel can be approached in a number of ways, including the following.

- **Subcontract** This has been discussed under the different headings throughout this chapter, but it is important that the SME is conscious of timescales here. Subcontracting for the short term is one thing, but doing so in the long term can damage the business' core competence – that is, the reason the company's goods and services are bought. You also need to consider whether it will create quality problems or make the company vulnerable if the subcontractor's business fails.

- **Part-time employment** Using part-time staff often has implications for the skills base of the organisation, which must be analysed.
- **Interim employment** For specific projects, the employment of staff on short-term contracts reduces costs.

■ Grants and support

Every company should investigate the potential for collaboration with grant-supplying organisations. Such organisations can help with the development of the organisation in terms of funding training, recruitment and so on.

■ New technology and improvements in personnel management

Software packages can produce staff appraisals, develop effective recruitment programmes, create and monitor organisational structures and develop and monitor training sessions.

CASE STUDY **Brainstorm, part IX**

The directors consider that the culture of the organisation is very positive with regard to the services the company provides – individuals are flexible, committed to education and enthusiastic about education and educational services.

Many of the problems of the company – its failure to exploit interest groups, for example – are due, in part, to inadequate direction and review. Introducing a more sophisticated review system, involving better recruitment, training and appraisals, would be likely to improve this area of company performance without the need for major additional expenditure.

The company is failing to provide adequate information, and so when promotions are made they are not thrown open to the entire workforce, but decided arbitrarily. The directors feel that, with the increased profitability of the company, working conditions can be improved. For example, the company could give staff access to low-cost dental services (arranged so as not to interfere with trading hours) and provide table-top vending machines for free coffee and tea.

FINANCIAL PLANNING IMPROVEMENTS

■ Cash flow

Here is a list of possible low-cost changes that can be made to improve the SME's current cash flow:

- invoice as soon as possible – if the contract is a lengthy one, ensure that you are able to invoice as the work progresses, say, monthly;
- establish rapid payment systems (using banks' transfer systems) with established customers wherever possible;
- keep bank accounts under daily control – pay money in as quickly as possible and transfer balances to deposit accounts or back to maintain balances;
- advise the bank well in advance of borrowing requirements and re-negotiate funding requirements to ensure that penalty interest is not charged to the account;
- deal with customer complaints immediately, so that there is no bar to payment;
- offer discounts for rapid payment, and institute a rigorous standard credit control system that is the responsibility of a single individual;
- investigate the possibility of using factoring companies to aid in the pre-payment of bills, but note that this option needs to be treated with caution, limited to certain key customers and, if possible, large invoices;
- pay fixed bills by instalments, if you can;
- consider stabilising revenues in fluctuating markets by hedging or buying forward;
- renegotiate terms and conditions with suppliers wherever possible, when business relationships permit;
- consider leasing rather than buying equipment if the cash flow is strong;
- use part-time labour and interim management to deal with peaks in demand and particular projects requiring specific expertise;
- consider potential changes in the fixed-cost component of pay, by introducing a bonus scheme.

■ Profit and loss

Here are some options you might like to consider.

- Reduce the cost of finance by means of long-term loans or new equity. There is often substantial equity funding available locally – many companies have developed a local shareholding 'angel' group of people who are loyal and undemanding, seeing it as important to support local companies.
- Reduce the cost of finance by changing banking arrangements. With the increasing competitiveness between banks and other providers, new alternatives may provide finance for a substantially lower cost. Change of this type needs to be considered carefully, though, before its implementation.
- Reduce the cost of finance by carefully checking the level of interest and bank charges levied by the provider. Many surveys indicate that many businesses are overcharged by their banks.
- Explore how useful local trade associations or government agencies could be to you as a potential source of low-cost loan finance or grants for particular aspects of business development (new product development, health and safety, environmental management, training and so on).
- Invest in tax advice. The continually changing taxation legislation means that you need expert help, so buy the best if the company is facing a tax bill – it will usually be a very worthwhile investment.
- Change depreciation rates and/or other write-offs. Profitability can be substantially affected by the speed at which assets are depreciated. Altering the depreciation rate is one method for improving your profit and loss statement, and the capitalisation of new product development is another.

■ Balance sheet

The following can help improve the SME's balance sheet.

- **Invest in advice** Balance sheet presentation and structuring is a combination of presentation and reality – expert help is required to optimise the final document.

- **Use local investors to improve the company's equity position** There are often individuals within the locality who are interested in making small investments in local companies – advertise for it. Such investors do not expect large returns and are normally happy to see the business make small dividend payments and employ staff in the locality.

> *There are often individuals within the locality who are interested in making small investments in local companies – advertise and they will come to you.*

CASE STUDY

Softawater, part XV

Cash flow is the prime area of concern for Softawater because its products are seasonal – people drink more water in the summer. By negotiating payment terms with some of its suppliers, it would be possible to delay certain payments until the peak selling season, thereby improving cash flow in the periods when the level of sales is low.

The company is also considering using more interim management – especially in new product development, which would have a substantial impact on cash flow expenditure.

SUMMARY

This chapter has been about how to improve the current performance of an SME without investing large amounts, using the planning exercise to continuously monitor and control efficiency. This process has been called fine-tuning here, though it is also a consolidation strategy. Then, systematically, the various areas of company activity were re-examined, looking for areas of possible fine-tuning, including sales management, promotional planning, distribution/logistical planning, production, new product or service development, facilities, administration, personnel and finance.

In this chapter the customer is king and the various aspects of company activity have been looked at from the viewpoint of the customer. Using this approach, the company begins to be seen as an integrated whole so when, for example, discount management by the sales force was looked at, it can be appreciated – by the end of the chapter – that there will be implications in the cash flow and that while keeping them to a minimum, offering some discount for rapid payment bears the needs of the customer in mind. Similarly, servicing the customer by handling complaints immediately may also impact back on the cash flow.

Driving strategy

INTRODUCTION

Where is your SME going? This is the third part of the planning exercise mentioned at the beginning of Chapter 3 and now is the time to search for an answer. At this stage in the development of the business plan, it is possible to begin to go forward and feel more confident about making the plan SURE (see Chapter 2). Certain elements of the discussion are cross-referenced to earlier or later in the book, as relevant. This chapter moves you on from improving the effectiveness of your current operation, towards identifying opportunities for the future (see Figure 1.1, page 10).

QUESTIONS OF STRATEGY

It is important to understand that once you ask the question 'Where to?', you are talking about planning strategy, and that before answering that particular question, you must also be certain about your knowledge of the company, its markets and its competitors. Therefore, this part of the planning exercise involves working through a series of steps and a new set of questions to achieve this end.

- What are the major influences affecting the development of the company?
- What strategic options exist?
- What are the most viable options, given the forces acting on the company?
- Who should consider their viability?

It is important to understand that once you ask the question 'Where to?', you are talking about planning strategy, and that before answering that particular question, you must also be certain about your knowledge of the company, its markets and its competitors.

In looking for answers, the major issues are described. The analysis is then demonstrated in the case study material.

There are many methods that can be used to decide on the best strategy, many of which are complicated to interpret or to use. One of the most practical is to consider the interaction of strengths, weaknesses, opportunities and threats – a SWOT analysis. Another, explained in the following section, is to analyse the 'drivers'. Chapter 2 introduced the concepts of strengths and weaknesses as part of the initial approach to setting the broad objectives for the plan. View this as a first step in the discussion of strategy and as the beginning of a SWOT analysis.

I have been making the case that business planning involves looking at the firm as a whole. At the same time, you must be clear about exactly what the whole company is doing. For example, the discussion of fine-tuning in Chapter 4 is about improving the company's current position in the market without adding significantly to cost. In the discussion about managing markets and gaining competitive advantage in this chapter, the planning horizon has altered – now the focus is starting to shift towards looking ahead to the medium- and long-term future.

INFLUENCES ON THE COMPANY – THE CONCEPT OF DRIVERS

Over the chosen planning horizon, the company needs to identify the major forces that will drive it – backwards, forwards, up and down. Essentially, this is another version of the SWOT. What each driver listed in Table 5.1 does is provide assistance in identifying the current position of the SME and what is happening to change its environment. The importance of each element is indicated by the depth of shading.

Table 5.1   Drivers and the planning horizon

Drivers	Short term	Medium term	Long term
Market factors			
Competitive factors			
Customer factors			
Product/service quality			
Speed			
Suppliers			

THE MARKET

Market drivers are largely outside the control of the company, and have their effect in the medium and long term. They include the impact of legislation and economic, social and technological trends on the whole country or on a majority of industrial/service sectors. They can be subdivided into a number of broad areas.

■ Government policy

Government affects all businesses in a number of ways. Legislation can either restrict or expand particular market sectors. It sets the balance between direct and indirect taxation. Here, changes affect the demand for products and services, as well as influencing the underlying cash flow of the SME. For example, those servicing the health, education, police, fire, armed services and much of the construction sectors find that their markets are largely controlled by government expenditure patterns. Support grants, soft loans and the like for particular industries or areas are also a factor in the planning of companies to which they are relevant.

■ The economy

Broad influences are: growth rates, changes in disposable income and inflation. Economic conditions are important drivers for most companies. High rates of economic growth, for example, lead to a significantly greater demand for luxury goods. Good news for SMEs in such areas as handicrafts, furniture, gourmet catering, landscape gardening, classic cars and so on. Economic downturns, by contrast, are particularly severe for companies with high breakeven points. Thus higher levels of disposable income are important for leisure, financial services and many parts of the retail sector.

■ Social change

A host of social trends could be analysed under this heading, but you can get an idea of the breadth of it by taking a quick look at demographics, and social attitudes. Social change affects far more companies than might be thought.

House builders need to meet demographic changes – for example, ageing populations, smaller households, migration – just as much as the manufacturers of convenience foods and cruise-liner operators. Equally, specific sectors of the market can be rapidly influenced by changing attitudes – witness the explosive growth of vegetarianism over the past decade throughout Europe, partially as a response to environmental issues, partially to health concerns.

■ Technology

This can be summarised by speed of change and direction of change.

Technological change increasingly influences all companies; even those in the craft sector are affected. Increasingly, companies promote their products via the Internet.

Another factor to be taken into account is the direction of change.

⇨ **Market factors are high brick walls for company planning – they are painful and often difficult to climb.**

CASE STUDY **Softawater, part XVI**

The size of the water treatment sector has been growing rapidly since the beginning of the decade and is heavily influenced by market drivers. Consumer demand has been growing at 8 per cent per annum, and industrial demand by 12 per cent since 1980.

■ Legislation for purer water has had a significant effect on the industrial sector, with the 'polluter pays' principle becoming more strongly established at both national and European levels. Purer water legislation could be considered a negative factor affecting consumer consumption, but this is more than offset by other market factors.

- Taxation rates have remained stable for all products, and there is no indication of imminent changes in the tax environment.

- Government expenditure patterns have not affected the company in the past.

- Government support for industry and services includes substantial sums for the promotion of new products and services internationally. The company could take advantage of these resources as it is excluded from other grants, including those for training, equipment and premises.

- Economic growth has not significantly increased or decreased the sale of water filtration systems.

- There is a strong and continuing relationship between increases in disposable income and the growth of the domestic water treatment market.

- Inflation has remained stable and has not adversely or positively affected the company.

- Demographic changes have had a substantial impact on the demand for water filters. An ageing population purchases more water filters.

- Social change has been perhaps the most important market driver – there is a growing awareness of what pure water should consist of and the inability of the current water supply system to provide it.

- Speed of change has been most dramatic in the development of industrial systems, while domestic systems have remained fairly traditional.

- The direction of change in the industrial systems has been to move towards mechanical methods of separation (by means of diffusion and osmosis), while chemical treatment remains the dominant approach in domestic systems.

These market drivers have been summarised in chart form by the directors of Softawater, as they affect their consumer (C) and industrial (I) ranges, with ticks for positive drivers and crosses for negative ones (Table 5.2).

Table 5.2   Market drivers for Softawater

Driver	Strength	Weakness	Opportunity	Threat
Legislation	✓✓(I)		✓✓(I)	
Taxation				
Expenditure				
Support			✓✓(I)✓✓(C)	
Growth				
Income	✓✓(C)			
Inflation				
Demography	✓✓(C)		✓✓(C)	
Social change	✓✓✓(C)		✓✓✓(C)	
Technology		✗✗ (I)	✓(I)	✗✗ (I)
Direction		✗✗ (I)	✓(I)	✗✗ (I)

The analysis suggests that the market drivers are largely positive for the consumer product range, but there are potential problems in maintaining a presence in the industrial sector.

Benchmark

One company in the consumer sector, Aqua, has been particularly effective in expanding sales by concentrating on the health aspects of pure water rather than the purity of the product itself. The major supplier of equipment to the industrial sector – Wasser from Germany – has invested heavily in developing new technology that will both lower the cost of water treatment and increase the volumes that could be purified.

THE COMPETITIVE ENVIRONMENT

Knowing your competitive environment involves measuring the strength and level of activity of other firms in the specific sector in which your company operates. The more competitive and demanding the market, the more detailed your understanding of it needs to be. Drivers in this category can be subdivided into a number of areas and should be considered more appropriate for medium- to long-term planning.

■ Market size and stage of growth

This changes continually, so that, over time, it expands or stabilises or declines – often under the influence of one or more of the market drivers discussed in the preceding section. Large markets are more complex – 'segmented' in marketing speak – than small ones. One example of segmentation is given in the section on market structure. As markets expand, new opportunities are created; as they decline, opportunities become less obvious, but they are still there.

The stage of a market's growth also provides indications as to the policy that the SME should follow – concentrating on expanding distribution in newly established markets, on product development when markets stabilise, and returning to controlling distribution in declining markets. The traditional concept is that markets have a standard pattern of expansion, maturity and then decline. In reality, each market is different and preconceptions about market change often lead to hasty actions.

■ The speed of market growth

This also gives a good idea about how competitive the market will be over the planning period. In rapidly growing markets, competitors often find it difficult to keep up with either the total volume of demand or the specific types of demand. This reduces the overall level of competitive pressure in the market. In a slowly growing or stable market, overcapacity tends to be normal, creating more pressure on prices.

■ Seasonality

Seasonality can be a severe competitive pressure in many sectors, with effects on cash flow, profitability, marketing and product development. The effect of seasonality on advertising was discussed in Chapter 4, in the section on promotion-related improvements.

■ Price elasticity or sensitivity

Price elasticity or sensitivity measures how competitive a market is. Where markets are highly price sensitive (butter, petrol, industrial feed stocks, building materials), an effective cost base is central to profitability and survival. Where price sensitivity is low (luxury products, financial services), profitability can be significantly improved by adding value to the product or service. Price sensitivity should not be considered appropriate for short-term change. You cannot simply tell a customer one day that you think they should pay 10 per cent more for your goods or services!

▒ *How to calculate price sensitivity*

Calculate the weighted market average price for each market period. For the example given below, the weighted market average price is 73, calculated on the basis of relative market shares.

Product	Market share percentage	Price	Market share × price
A	10	90	900
B	30	80	2400
C	40	70	2800
D	20	60	1200
Total	**100**	**73**	**7300**

Movements of price and volumes against the market average are either steep – indicating high price sensitivity – or flatter – suggesting that the product or service is less price-sensitive. In practical terms, the SME needs to be aware of the degree of price sensitivity rather than the absolute figure.

■ Market structure and market position

This tells the business planner clearly what freedom the SME has in the market to develop specific policies. Markets will vary from ones that are highly structured, with one or two major suppliers, to those that are highly fragmented.

In a highly structured market, the market leaders will dominate pricing, product policy, promotion and distribution. Other companies within such markets have to be highly focused to survive and prosper.

In a fragmented market, a wider range of policies can be followed by the majority of companies. Most markets will have:

- market leaders, maintaining their position by high levels of new product development, investment in production plant and the major distribution channels;
- market challengers, attempting to out-compete the market leaders in areas of their market activity by concentrating on certain distribution outlets or methods and price/promotional competition;
- market specialists, concentrating on narrow market sectors with specialist and differentiated products or services;
- commodity manufacturers, producing market-standard products and competing purely on price, with a low cost base.

■ Market coverage

Market coverage means how well-established companies are servicing the market. Market gaps may exist that can be used by smaller, more agile competitors. New ways of getting to the market will create new opportunities. The level of market coverage will also be influenced by whether or not there are likely to be any new competitors or 'market entrants'.

■ Competitive product or service supply position

▥ *Logistics*

Here you must again consider planning horizons. Short-term issues are discussed in Chapter 4. Here, the focus is on the longer-term, or strategic possibility, of gaining competitive advantage by investing larger amounts in better distribution.

Different physical distribution methods may enable a company to gain competitive advantage by choosing a route that meets customer supply requirements better than others or creates a significant cost saving. For example, with the changes occurring in the European Union, many companies, both in the manufacturing and service sectors, are re-evaluating their physical distribution policies to gain competitive advantage. Such moves are longer-term, as they involve a whole series of logistical issues and require substantial investment – where to site warehouses, additional production points, stockholding, integrated order processing from a variety of locations and so on (see also Chapter 4, under Distribution/logistical improvements, and Table 5.3).

Table 5.3   Competitive position of the distribution system

Issues	Competitive position	Investment required	Timescale
Physical distribution			
Inventory			
Warehousing			
Order processing			

■ Substitutes

The price sensitivity and the competitive position of the product is also affected by the availability of a substitute product or service. Substantial increases in the price of your product or service may mean that substitutes are purchased in preference or that competitors improve the quality and acceptability of their substitute products. Where a company has a product or service that has few or ineffective substitutes, it will be able to gain far greater competitive advantage.

■ Promotional policy

An analysis of promotional policy will indicate how well the company is performing against the competition. The measurement criteria must be the effectiveness of the promotional policy in achieving its objectives and the cost per sale compared with the competition.

Table 5.6   Comparative production position

Issues	Competitive position	Investment required	Timescale
Plant capacity			
Plant flexibility			
Sophistication			
Age			
In-house manufacture			
Production skills			

■ Competitive personnel issues

How the company is organised, the skills and productivity of the staff – all influence the competitive position of the firm. Some of the solutions to short-term problems were given in Chapter 4, but the overall position of the company should be reviewed in relation to that of the competition. The main components are shown in Table 5.7.

Table 5.7   Comparative personnel analysis

Issues	Competitive position	Investment required	Timescale
Structure			
Staff			
Skills			
Systems			
Shared values			
Support			
Style			

■ Competitive financial position

The creation of an effective information system and the introduction of short-term improvements discussed in Chapters 3 and 4 do not reveal the full picture of how effectively the company is managing financially. Poorly managed finances restrict strategic options, while healthy finances mean that strategic options are considerably enhanced (Table 5.8).

Table 5.8 Comparative financial position

Issues	Competitive position	Investment required	Timescale
Gross profit			
ROCE			
Cost per unit			
Fixed costs			
DER			
Liquidity ratio			

▷ **If your company cannot establish competitive advantage, it should not compete.**

CASE STUDY **Brainstorm, part X**

Let us look at how these issues translate into Brainstorm's situation.

- **Stage of market growth** The market for educational toys and games has been expanding rapidly since 1980 and shows few signs of stabilising. The implication for Brainstorm is that there will be a number of new customers in the market that have still not been effectively reached.
- **Size of competitors** Brainstorm faces two large competitors and many other suppliers. However, the market for educational toys can still be described as fragmented. The implication for Brainstorm is that it can still expand without significant competitive counter-action.
- **Market position** Brainstorm is well established in its local market area, where it could be considered a market leader. Regionally, it is a market challenger, and nationally a niche specialist.
- **Seasonality** Brainstorm, like all toy retailers, suffers from the problems of seasonality. The market position the company occupies insulates it to an extent, though only when the group can generate effective revenues from interest groups.
- **Price sensitivity** Brainstorm has found that pricing is not a major constraint to product purchase. This has allowed the company to introduce higher-priced and more profitable products.

- **Substitutes** Although there are several other child-related products and services that parents spend money on, research shows that 'education'-related products are perceived as a distinct category, with no clear substitutes.
- **Market coverage** Brainstorm has clearly demonstrated that market coverage is limited and there are substantial opportunities in dealing direct with specific interest groups.
- **Market entrants** Brainstorm does not believe that there will be any new market entrants during the period covered by the plan.
- **Logistics** The company in its service sector is not affected by physical distribution issues as suppliers deliver direct to each store.
- **Promotional policy** Brainstorm considers that it has the most effective promotional mix in the market, combining largely effective sales penetration with low-cost, but effective, sales promotional expenditure, and focused direct promotional investment.

Part-time staff have called on the majority of interest groups to make presentations about the educational value of the various products in the Brainstorm range. Approximately 60 per cent of the available market has been covered in this way, with representatives making two presentations to each group per year on average. The company also has skilled sales staff in the retail shops, who are more knowledgeable than those in competitors' shops, and able to provide a higher level of service.

The company provides a number of discount cards to schools and playgroups that enable them to receive free equipment, provided parents shop at the stores and fill in the cards. It also carries out highly effective direct mail, sending children whose parents shop in participating stores a birthday and Christmas card, both of which contain a voucher to be used towards a future purchase.

- **Personnel position** The company is strong, compared to its competitors, regarding its staff and skills. However, information flow and motivation are better handled elsewhere.
- **Financial position** The company is one of the strongest in the sector. It achieves high profit margins, good returns on capital employed, has low fixed costs, no debt and a high level of liquidity. Financial restrictions are not going to significantly limit its strategic options (Table 5.9).

Table 5.9 Brainstorm's SWOT analysis

Issues	Strengths	Weaknesses	Opportunities	Threats
Market growth			✓✓	
Competitor size		✗✗		✗✗
Market position				
Seasonality		✗✗	✓✓	
Substitutes	✓✓			
Price	✓✓		✓✓	
Market coverage	✓✓		✓✓	
Market entrants				
Logistics				
Promotion policy	✓✓		✓✓	
Sales policy	✓✓		✓✓	
Personnel	✓✓		✓✓	
Finances	✓✓		✓✓	

Benchmark

Brainstorm used a highly successful games retailer as its main comparison. This company has been one of the most profitable over the past five years, by following a policy of locating in large conurbations with or without existing competition, concentrating on knowledgeable staff, a continually changing product range of the latest releases and promoting via the various clubs that exist for games and game development.

The games retailer also has a well-organised personnel policy, with strong internal promotion, good information flow and a good motivational plan.

CUSTOMERS

Customer drivers relate to the structure of the customer base and how the company can develop profitable business. Understanding who customers are, what types and quality of products or services are wanted by them, when they want them, and how they buy them, enables companies to gain competitive advantage. Maintaining the customer base is crucial to the continued success of the company.

■ Customer types

Classification by type of customer produces different approaches in consumer and industrial sectors. It is sensible to identify consumer goods' customers by demographic criteria (age, sex, household size, location), socio-economic (social class or stage in lifecycle), and psychographic (attitudes). Industrial customers can be separated into categories such as size, type of technology, type of operation, location.

> *Understanding who customers are, what types and quality of products or services are wanted by them, when they want them, and how they buy them, enables companies to gain competitive advantage.*

■ Customer dependency

Businesses are also driven by their reliance on certain customers. One of the major causes of SME failure is dependency on a limited customer base. Most companies find that the 80/20 rule holds true throughout their growth and expansion – that is, that 80 per cent of their business will be derived from 20 per cent of their customer base. However, there is a significant difference between 1 out of 5 customers accounting for 80 per cent of the business and 30 out of 150. For some, the cost of increasing the customer base may be prohibitive, but for many the costs are relatively low.

■ Customer stability

The stability of the customer base also influences strategy. A well-established, loyal customer base – ideally tied to the company via trade marketing agreements (Chapter 4, Table 4.7) – is a source of strategic strength. Where the customer base is continually changing, strategic development becomes more difficult.

■ Buying methods and group pressures

How customers buy their products is particularly important for industrial products and for expensive consumer goods. Buying methods are generally straightforward for low-cost consumer items, but more analysis and discussion takes place when deciding about more expensive items, such as durables, cars and houses. For the industrial customer, there will often be a formal buying process, with an individual or committee involved in the decision making. An effective mechanism for managing these complicated buying arrangements is vital for companies operating in these sectors.

As the price increases, so does the level of perceived risk. It is important to understand how customers reach their buying decisions to reduce the perceived level of risk. The latter is substantially increased if there are any group pressures in the buying decision. This is most common in the industrial sector, but is also apparent in the purchase of many consumer goods, especially fashion and toys.

  Establishing a new customer costs, on average, seven times more than maintaining an existing one.

CASE STUDY   ## Softawater, part XVII

- **Types of customers** Softawater services both consumer and industrial markets. The customers in the consumer market are typically female, from affluent households, aged 35 plus. The industrial customers vary considerably in size, type of manufacturing operation, location and type of technology used. The industrial market is, therefore, far more complicated for Softawater than is the consumer market, with a greater need to define the product and service provided. Softawater has found that medium-sized companies operating in the canning or bottling industry are particularly responsive targets for their larger industrial unit.

- **Customer reliance** The company has significantly reduced its reliance on single customers, with one major supermarket group now comprising 15 per cent of its sales when, two years ago, this customer accounted for 40 per cent of sales.

- **Customer stability** The company has a number of stable customers, with good working relationships. The introduction of trade marketing agreements would further stabilise the existing customer base.

- **Buying methods** With the low cost of the consumer unit, the majority of customers perceive little risk in the purchase. For the industrial units – selling at between £300 and £1500, depending on the exact configuration – the risks are considerably greater, and the company has yet to develop an effective method of trial to help overcome this problem.

■ **Group pressures** For the consumer product, few group pressures exist. In the industrial sector, group pressures are far more marked, and the company has still not developed a sales policy that copes effectively with this problem (Table 5.10).

Table 5.10 Softawater's SWOT analysis for customers

Issues	Strengths	Weaknesses	Opportunities	Threats
Type	✓✓ (C)	✓✓ (I)	✓✓ (C)	
Reliance	✓✓ (C)			
Methods	✓✓ (C)	✓✓ (I)		
Pressure		✓✓ (I)		

Benchmark

Softawater benchmarked a successful cafetière manufacturer and its leading competitor, Aqua, in the consumer market. In the industrial sector, it chose an American manufacturer of industrial cleaning equipment. This company has been very successful in penetrating the European market by manufacturing low-cost demonstration units that show the benefits of the system without the full operating potential. These units can be left on site for prolonged periods and then sales can be achieved on the back of the attractiveness of the basic proposition.

PRODUCT OR SERVICE QUALITY

Chapters 3 and 4 have touched on various aspects of product or service quality in the context of the planning information system and short-term, low-cost improvements. Although there are short-term improvements that can be introduced in this area, the majority of changes are medium- to long-term as they require investment in equipment, personnel or product or service development. Product or service quality drives the perception of the company within the market, the price customers will pay and the rate at which the SME can become established.

■ The benefits bundle

Marketers say that a product is a 'bundle of benefits'. We rarely buy a product or a service for a single factor, but more often for a combination.

For a manufactured product, techni-cal factors, such as size, weight, colour, performance, combine with the non-technical, such as availability, technical support, spare parts. Within the industrial sector, non-technical

Product or service quality drives the perception of the company within the market, the price customers will pay and the rate at which the SME can become established.

benefits are often at least as important as technical ones – the consumer sector is dominated by technical benefits.

Service product benefits vary from sector to sector and can only be defined in the context of that sector. For example, retailing benefit is achieved by the combination of location, internal design, product width, product depth. Airlines' benefit, by contrast, is achieved by means of destinations, departure times, reliability, baggage handling, ease of checking in.

Both manufactured and service products also provide attitudinal benefits. People buy products and services because they provide satisfaction of certain kinds – feelings of security, superiority or whatever. For consumer products, attitudinal benefits in many sectors are vital (perfumes and fashion, for example), but they are also important in the industrial sector, as confidence in the product or service is often a vital element in buying behaviour.

The price benefit is a combination of how the other benefits are measured, and often a benefit in itself – especially in luxury goods and sophisticated industrial equipment.

Quality certification has also become an often important part of the product or product service benefit. Standardisation and controls in the form of ISO 9000 or ISO 14000 (as a necessary part of the product or service benefit) is an option that needs to be given serious consideration. The value of such certification processes will depend on the customer mix and the competitive nature of the industry.

▨ *The innovation bundle*

With an increasingly competitive environment, changing the bundle of benefits (or innovating) becomes an increasingly important driver for achieving competitive advantage. The reality is that innovation covers a much wider range of product change than typically accepted, from the major to the minor (Table 5.11).

Table 5.11 Strategic options and planning horizons in innovation

Types of innovation	Description
Sector creating innovation – long term	New materials, concepts
Performance improvement – medium term	Improving output from existing concept
Process – medium term	Making products more effectively
Technological reorganisation – medium term	Combining technologies into new products
Reformulation – short term	Recombining existing ingredients in a new way
Branding – medium term	Changing perceptions to the product or service via promotion
Design – short term	Changing the external shape or control surfaces
Service – short term	Altering the way in which the customer is served
Packaging – short term	Improving the presentation and storage capability of the product

▨ *Product viability*

A useful method for appraising the investment requirements for each product, or service, is to carry out a product viability analysis. This looks forward from the current position, analyses the forces acting on the product or service over the short, medium and long term, and evaluates potential solutions where there are problems (Table 5.12).

What such an analysis does is assess, in a simple, practical way, whether or not the product is capable of improvement with investment – it does not presuppose that products are going to follow a particular pattern of growth and decline, which is the common problem with the other forecasting system used in this context – the product lifecycle. Some companies have a tradition of effective new product development, while others do not and need to give time to implementing techniques for managing this type of change. Assuming that the age of a product will determine its future would appear fatalistic to many leading companies.

Table 5.12 Product viability planning for one product

Pressure	Short term	Medium term	Long term	Solutions
Legislation				
Economic				
Social				
Technological				
Competitive change				
Technical benefit				
Non-technical				
Attitudinal				
Price				

⇨ **Poor products or services will, typically, be mentioned to 20 contacts, good service to three.**

CASE STUDY

Softawater, part XVIII

Softawater has product quality advantages in its consumer product. The filtration system lasts longer than that of its competitors and is priced more aggressively. All other pressures regarding the planning cycle are limited – legislation on pure water is unlikely to impact the product, economic growth will enhance purchases of the product, social trends are positive, with far greater numbers of individuals being interested in the purity of their drinking water than in the past.

The technology is slowly changing, with new resins replacing the older systems. This does not pose a particular threat as new resins are available from a number of suppliers. The company still has limited distribution, and the majority of customers are unaware of the benefits that the consumer product can provide.

It is in the industrial systems that product quality and viability are most under pressure. Softawater knows it has problems in all areas of its product offerings in the industrial sector – technical, non-technical, attitudinal and price. It consistently lags behind competitors in terms of the sophistication of its technology – with German and American competitors producing new, more energy-efficient systems that are quicker and more cost-effective. There is a clear prospect of new technologies becoming available that will further weaken the competitive position of the company.

The pricing of the industrial system is a problem as the high costs of the bought-in components make it difficult for the company to price aggressively and achieve adequate profit margins.

Softawater is not certified for either ISO 9000 or ISO 14000. This is not a problem in the consumer sector, but it is an issue that is becoming more important in relation to servicing the industrial market, especially when dealing with larger clients and any with overseas operations (Table 5.13).

Table 5.13   Softawater's competitive position with regard to product quality

Issues	Strengths	Weaknesses	Opportunities	Threats
Technological benefit	✓✓ (C)	*XX*(I)	✓✓ (C)	*XX* (I)
Non-technological		✓✓ (C) *XX* (I)	✓✓ (C)	
Attitudinal		✓✓ (C) *XX* (I)	✓✓ (C)	
Certification		*XX* (I)		*XX* (I)
Price	✓✓ (C)	*XX* (I)		
Innovation		*XX* (I)	*XX* (I)	*XX* (I)

Benchmark

Softawater benchmarked itself against its major competitor, Aqua. Aqua has successfully exploited the consumer market with its sales and promotion policy, which has built a strong, non-technical benefit (distribution availability) and attitudinal benefit (brand identification) in the market.

The industrial leader, Wasser, is Softawater's benchmark for successful product development. Wasser has a strong engineering and research department, which is able to identify new product concepts and bring them rapidly to market. Wasser is also certified for both ISO 9000 and ISO 14000.

SPEED

In a competitive environment, speed of operation is vital to success. Most of the investment will be medium to long-term.

Speed throughout the SME is a separate issue – speed of response to enquiries and complaints, new product development, information transfer and so on are all important. Speed of response adds to the dimension of product quality as a method of building effective business relationships. Speed will also often generate higher margins and lower fixed costs.

Speed has positive effects on all of the following aspects of the business.

- **Customer service** Fast customer service builds customer loyalty.
- **Information** Fast information (provided it is simple, accurate and useful) enables the company to respond quickly to opportunities and manage potential problems.
- **Decision making** Fast decision making complements a fast information system.
- **Production** Speed substantially reduces working capital requirements and tends to provide higher levels of service to the customer.
- **New product development** Increasing the speed of new product development creates competitive advantage in that an innovative product that is first to market generally becomes the market leader. A final advantage for companies speeding up their product development is that the planning horizon can shorten, making the planning process more effective and controllable.

⇨ **Shorter production cycles and faster customer response have been central to the success of many organisations.**

Brainstorm, part XI

Brainstorm has spent considerable time on setting standards for the speed of its service. Customers are to be greeted within two minutes of entering the store, telephone enquiries within four rings; shelves are to be restocked twice a day; the store is to be cleaned once a day; window displays are to be changed weekly; letters are to be answered within two days, and any mail order enquiry is to be despatched within three (subject to payment) (Table 5.14).

The company's information system is basic, recording products that are sold via a barcode system, which identifies these for accounting purposes. There is no link to stock, and reordering is carried out via physical stock checks at the end of each week. The decision-making process for promotional expenditure, sales policy and the employment of part-time staff is all centralised, and store managers find that it is often difficult to get decisions on things quickly enough to meet the needs of the business.

New product development is also part of the company's plan. It allocates approximately 20 per cent of its selling space to new products and trains the staff at three-monthly intervals on the value of each item. The company is on the mailing lists of all major suppliers and receives regular streams of samples. The two directors also attend the major toy fairs.

Table 5.14 Brainstorm's SWOT analysis of its customer service drivers

Issues	Strengths	Weaknesses	Opportunities	Threats
Customer service	✓✓			
Information		*XX*	✓✓	
Decision making		*XX*	✓✓	
Production				
New product development	✓✓		✓✓	

Benchmark

Brainstorm has concentrated on the way in which fast food outlets handle their customers, where action standards are set for speed and quality of service. These outlets set action standards for the entire range of customer service issues – speed of service, length of eye contact, complementary sales, product availability. Brainstorm has not set benchmarks for information management or decision-making processes.

SUPPLIERS

As businesses become more specialised and concentrate on their core competence – that is, the activity that provides them with competitive advantage and separates them from the competition – the importance of suppliers has increased. Maintaining a network of effective suppliers has become another method of gaining competitive advantage. Working with suppliers to develop an effective interrelationship will, on the whole, be a medium- to long-term investment, although any short-term improvements that can be made must not be ignored (see also Chapter 4). By concentrating on the following, SMEs can improve their overall performance:

- speed;
- quality;
- reliability;
- cost of supply.

⇨ **Effective supplier relations can add up to 5 per cent to gross profit margins for the average SME.**

CASE STUDY **Softawater, part XIX**

Softawater uses distinct types of suppliers for the two types of water filter it manufactures (see Table 5.15).

Table 5.15 Softawater's SWOT analysis of its supplier drivers

Issues	Strengths	Weaknesses	Opportunities	Threats
Speed	✓✓(I)(C)			
Quality	✓✓ (C)	✗✗(I)		
Reliability	✓✓ (C)			
Price	✓✓ (C)	✗✗(I)	✗✗(I)	

The company purchases raw materials for its domestic filter systems and converts them in-house to the finished product. There are over 12 suppliers to choose from that can provide the quality of raw materials required when it is wanted. As the supply industry is highly price competitive, there is little flexibility in negotiating improved prices, although, obviously, as Softawater's volumes grow they are able to achieve higher levels of discounts.

The industrial product is brought in as components and these are assembled within the factory. There are problems with the quality of the components as the suppliers do not have access to the latest technology. The costs of these components have remained fairly high, and it is possible that some of the other potential suppliers in the Far East could provide the same quality products for a lower price.

Benchmark

Softawater has not benchmarked itself against any competitor in the industry for consumer products as they all operate within the same limitations of the international supplier market.

The industrial benchmark is considered to be Diatron, a manufacturer of state-of-the-art diagnostic equipment. Diatron maintains a complex network of subcontractors throughout the Pacific Rim and manages to keep its product technologically advanced by designing and manufacturing a small percentage of products in-house that it cannot source elsewhere or by designing products for manufacture outside the company.

THE STRATEGIC OPTIONS

Having completed a review of the main driving forces acting on the company, the business planner can identify the most viable options for the business. These broadly defined options are often called strategy, and they establish, in general terms, what policy the company should be following. Refresh your memory by looking back to Chapter 2 where an analysis of broad and specific objectives for the key decision makers was completed.

As with all general issues, there are often problems associated with the creation of strategy.

First is the generality of strategy. The statement that the strategy of the firm should be to expand outside its current geographical base is all very well, but what does it mean in practical terms? Which market? How? When? You can see this from the exercise in Chapter 2, but it is clear that these broad questions are being used to help SME managers clarify their broad strategies and design a planning information system in Chapter 3 that helps them to act to achieve these goals. And the approach taken in this book to the business planning cycle has been to establish the broad objectives before getting down to specifics (Figure 1.1).

Second, in the real world, most companies will be following a mixture of strategies for particular parts of their product range or operation, creating further complexity.

Third, strategic analysis rarely takes account of the basic issues confronting the company. Do we really want to grow, are we prepared to take the riskier route? Again, I hope that by incorporating elements of SWOT analysis, I have helped to demonstrate, from the very start of the discussion, how it is possible for the business planner to use strategic analysis to its best advantage.

Table 5.16 outlines certain strategic options that might be before an SME once it has completed an analysis of the various market influences covered in the first part of this chapter.

Table 5.16   Strategic options, their risks and timescales

Options	Descriptions	Risks and timescales
No action	Current operation meets all objectives	Nil, short term
Consolidation	Improving profitability while retaining customers	Low, short term
Withdrawal	Closure of operation	Low, short term
Market penetration	More of current range to current customer type	Low, medium term
Market development	New markets for existing products	Moderate, medium term
Product development	New products for existing customer base	High, medium term
Diversification	New products in new markets	Very high, medium to long term

The strategic planning idea that there is a 'golden circle' of market penetration, market development and product development should be the ideal standard for all companies, whether they are large or small (Figure 5.1).

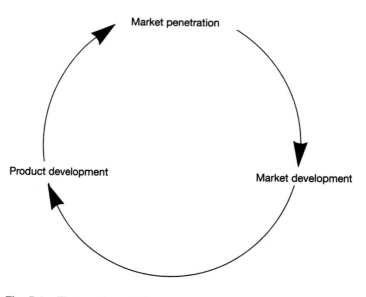

Fig. 5.1 The golden circle

CASE STUDY **Softawater, part XX**

Softawater has a fairly strong base from which to expand, although there are many strategic problems that need to be resolved in the light of the analysis of the forces driving the company.

It is clear that three broad options need to be addressed:

- expanding the current customer base with the existing product;
- gaining competitive advantage in the industrial sector via product development;
- reorganising the company in certain areas by means of consolidation so that a more effective operating base can be created (see Table 5.17).

Table 5.17 Softawater's strategic options

		Strengths	Weaknesses
		■ Growing market ■ Few legal restrictions ■ Good market profitability ■ Stable customer base ■ Good cost of product ■ Good consumer product quality ■ Good speed of production ■ Good revenue stream	■ Limited customer base ■ Strong competition in industrial market ■ Poor promotional policy ■ Poor industrial product quality ■ Poor industrial component suppliers ■ Poor cost base ■ Poor product development history ■ Poor personnel policy
Opportunities	■ Take more of growing market ■ Improve profitability ■ Become market leader in key segments	**Market penetration** **Product development**	**Consolidation**
Threats	■ New competitors ■ New technology	**Market penetration** **Product development**	

CASE STUDY | **Brainstorm, part XII**

Brainstorm's analysis suggests that the company could take advantage of the growing demand for educational toys. The company has a strong competitive position in its local area, although its marketing policies are not as effective as they might be.

The company has weaknesses in its organisational structure, information systems and decision-making processes, but achieves good product quality and high rates of innovation. The revenue streams are well established via its retail stores, although sourcing other customers has not been fully developed; the cost base is simple and well controlled.

The conclusion from the strategic analysis is that the company is well placed to carry out a policy of market penetration (see Table 5.18).

Table 5.18   Brainstorm's strategic options

			Strengths	**Weaknesses**
			■ Growing market ■ Governmental policies positive ■ Fragmented market with few local competitors ■ Good market profitability ■ Stable customer base ■ Good product quality ■ Good revenue streams ■ Controlled cost base ■ Good finances ■ Good personnel	■ Seasonality ■ Information systems ■ Distribution channels ■ Decision making ■ Motivational policy
Opportunities	■ Grow with market		**Market penetration** **Market development**	**Market penetration** **Consolidation**
Threats	■ Competitive arrival ■ Change in governmental policy		**Market penetration** **Product development**	

■ Choosing a strategy

It is important, at an early stage, to identify those strategies that have a chance of success and discard those that, realistically, cannot be effective. The mere fact of defining a potential strategy does not mean that it will work. First, a strategy may fail because the detailed information on the viability of the strategy will prove its unacceptability. Second, the resource implications of the strategy may mean that it cannot work, or at best, has a high probability of failure.

Different strategies have substantially different impacts. Product development and diversification are generally the most demanding, while a do-nothing or withdrawal strategy requires far lower resources. Impacts on personnel, production and other factors will also vary significantly, with the main areas of importance illustrated in Table 5.19.

Table 5.19   Resource implications of strategic development – the more stars the greater the impact

Impact	Do nothing	Withdrawal	Consolidate	Market penetration	Market development	Product development	Diversification
Investment		*	*	**	***	****	****
Cash flow		*	**	**	***	****	*****
Short-term profitability		*	**	**	***	***	****
Short-term return on capital employed		*	*	*	**	***	****
Production capacity		*		*	**	*	***
Production flexibility		*			**	***	***
Production sophistication		*			**	***	***
Supplier base		*	*	*	**	***	****
Staff		***	***	*	**	***	*****
Skills			*	*	***	***	****
Structure		**	**	*	***	**	****
Shared values		***	***		*	*	***
Style		**	**		**	**	***
Information systems		*	*	*	***	***	****

Using these tables enables you to filter the options available by ranking the chances of achieving the desired strategy on a scale of 1 to 10 – 10 indicating complete availability of resources required for implementation and 1 indicating extremely limited resources. As a rough guide, this indicates the chances of success of the strategy, with a score of 100 indicating a 100 per cent chance of success.

The advantage of this system is that it is quick and simple and is not resource-intensive. It also allows the company to use time more effectively by concentrating on those strategic elements that are viable.

Table 5.20   Areas to be evaluated in choosing strategy options

Issues	Strategy 1	Strategy 2	Strategy 3
Meets broad objectives	10	5	
Meets specific objectives	10		
Acceptability	10	5	
People	10	5	
Production	10	3	
Logistics	10	2	
Suppliers	10	6	
Information system	10	8	
Finance	10	2	
Marketing	10	4	
Total	100	40	

CASE STUDY **Softawater, part XXI**

The view of the members of the planning team is that Softawater faces major problems in implementing a product development strategy over the planning horizon because of problems in key areas.

Market penetration and consolidation, by contrast, achieve far higher scores in their evaluation. They conclude that the company needs to take time to build product development capability within the organisation prior to embarking on investment in this area.

Market penetration is likely to be the policy that best meets the broad and specific objectives of the company and will be most acceptable to the major interest groups within the organisation (Table 5.21).

Table 5.21 Softawater's strategy evaluation

Issues	Market penetration	Consolidation	Product development
Meets broad objectives	8	7	3
Meets specific objectives	8	7	4
Acceptability	8	5	4
People	8	10	2
Production	10	10	6
Logistics	10	10	6
Suppliers	10	10	2
Information system	10	8	5
Finance	6	8	1
Marketing	7	6	5
Total	85	81	38

CASE STUDY

Brainstorm, part XIII

By contrast Brainstorm faces few potential implementation problems with its proposed market penetration policy. It will also be able to solve other issues via consolidation. Market penetration is the policy that best meets the broad and specific objectives of the company and will also be the most acceptable (Table 5.22).

Table 5.22 Brainstorm's strategy evaluation

Issues	Market penetration	Consolidation
Meets broad objectives	8	4
Meets specific objectives	8	5
Acceptability	8	5
People	8	8
Production	10	10
Logistics	10	10
Suppliers	10	10
Information system	6	8
Finance	10	10
Marketing	7	10
Total	85	80

ALLOCATING RESPONSIBILITIES FOR EVALUATION OF
STRATEGIC OPTIONS

Allocating responsibilities for the development of strategic options will mean that the planning group can rapidly identify those that can be discarded and create a broad understanding of the demands of the remaining strategies. To ensure continuity of planning, it will be important that those individuals who have been responsible to date for the development of the plan continue with it, and are responsible for the evaluation of the implications of the chosen action.

SUMMARY

This chapter provides guidance for those SME planners who are evaluating possible future directions for their company. As the discussion is about strategy, the emphasis is on marketing. The approach taken, however, is to give attention to detail. It shows SME managers why they must be confident and knowledgeable about the detail of the influences on their company – its markets, competitors, customers, products. It is this finely tuned knowledge that makes a realistic choice of strategy possible; it is the foundation of successful strategic planning.

The discussion uses the concept of drivers, but also adds to the SWOT analysis technique begun in Chapter 2. The case studies illustrate how the market information and these techniques are integrated into company planning.

The key market influences are related to various strategic options and further guidance is offered on the evaluation of different strategies. A range of strategic options is described. Also included is a filtering technique that helps you evaluate the most plausible options, a mechanism for evaluating whether or not these options are realistic and achievable and the resource implications of the strategies being considered.

Action from strategy

6

INTRODUCTION

Chapter 5 describes how the SME planner can analyse the forces driving the company and come to a broad conclusion about which strategies best meet the realities of the marketplace and whether they are, in general terms, feasible, realistic and meeting broad and specific objectives of a particular company. The next step, taken in this chapter, is to turn these considerations about possible best strategic options into a detailed assessment of whether initial thoughts stand up to more rigorous scrutiny when the specific actions necessary for the implementation of each strategy are considered. The business planner must now work through each of the main strategic options and quantify the implications.

Having identified the broad strategic options in Chapter 5, another structured analysis is required. It is practical to devote a phase to information collection, a phase to detailed analysis of the marketing, organisational and financial implications and a final element of considering how the strategy should be implemented – whether internally (organic) or via acquisition or in the form of a joint venture.

NEW INFORMATION REQUIREMENTS

All change leads to uncertainty. This uncertainty can be reduced or removed by a full understanding of how the SME will cope with change. This means that new, detailed information about a few strategies that appear most appropriate will have to be collected and integrated into the existing information system. As strategies become more complex, the SME will need to collect and analyse more and more details to enable it to perform the new tasks as effectively as possible.

All change leads to uncertainty. This uncertainty can be reduced or removed by a full understanding of how the SME will cope with change.

The specific information requirements will be components of the market 'drivers' identified in Chapter 5. The company's business planner needs to ask the following questions.

- **Market** What political, legislative, economic, environmental, social, technological and other issues are relevant to the new plan that were not considered in the old one?
- **Competition** What new competition/competitive structure will the firm be facing? Can we monitor the competition regularly?
- **Customer** What product and service gap will the new strategy fill? How can we measure the success or failure of how the firm provides this new service?
- **Product or service quality** What are the demands of the new market for product or service quality? Can we measure the success or failure of how the firm produces its products or services?
- **Speed** Will we need to speed processes to meet the demands of the new strategy?
- **Supplier** Will the suppliers required for the new strategy perform to expectations. Can we adequately control their performance?

As with the other exercises regarding information, the frequency of information collection may have to be re-evaluated and altered as a result. The company may also have to change the source of its information. For a well-established company in a stable market, most of the information requirements will come from internal sources and informal contacts with long-standing customers. When a company moves into new areas or products, however, it will have to look for a substantial quantity of information from external suppliers. These are the secondary sources discussed in Chapter 4 under administration improvements – databases, trade magazines, government publications. In certain cases, the company will have to invest in specific, tailored data collection – or primary information. As this is expensive, it is essential that the company clearly defines exactly what information is required, and the form in which it should be presented. The decisions made about what constitutes necessary information will determine the level of investment necessary to collect the information (Table 6.1).

⇨ **Specialised information is expensive, so be totally clear about what you want before commissioning it – list the information you want and the form in which you want it.**

Table 6.1 Identifying information needs for strategic action

Area	Factor	Importance	Frequency	Source
Market				
Competition				
Customer				
Product quality				
Speed				
Supplier				

Another kind of investment decision will be necessary for companies with long planning horizons. They will need to decide what type of forecasting system they put in place in order to model future trends (the main forecasting methods and their strengths and weaknesses were identified in Chapter 3).

CONSOLIDATION

All the elements of a consolidation strategy have been described in terms of fine-tuning in Chapter 4.

MARKET PENETRATION

Many of the elements of a market penetration strategy have been discussed in earlier chapters as, clearly, improving operating effectiveness in a consolidation strategy will often involve selling more products or services to the customer base. Those elements of earlier discussions that are relevant here are listed in Table 6.2, together with chapter references.

■ **Marketing issues**

Market penetration involves the sale of more products to the current customer base. It involves investment, but at a lower level than is the case for other routes. Working up from the least costly option to the most expensive – always keeping customers' requirements in mind – will normally be the simplest method of optimising this strategy.

> *Working up from the least costly option to the most expensive – always keeping customers' requirements in mind – will normally be the simplest method of optimising a market penetration strategy.*

Table 6.2 Elements of market penetration strategy discussed earlier and the types of action required to implement one

Area of activity	Action	Go to
Sales management	Sell more effectively, increase investment in sales force activity, motivate salesforce	Chapter 4 Chapter 6 Chapter 4
Sales promotion	Change techniques	Chapter 4
Media promotion	Promote more effectively	Chapters 4 and 6
Product	Quality control	Chapters 3, 4 and 5
Distribution channels	Higher levels of service, trade marketing agreements	Chapter 4 Chapter 4, Tables 4.1 and 4.7
Physical distribution	Increasing effectiveness, consider alternatives	Chapters 4 and 6
Logistical	Increased investment	Chapters 4 and 6
Order processing	Improve effectiveness	Chapter 4
Inventory levels	Change service levels	Chapter 4
Warehousing	Improve effectiveness	Chapter 4
Pricing	Discount	Chapter 4

There remain a number of areas of action that require increased investment, but need to be evaluated using different methods from those so far discussed.

■ Increasing investment in sales force activity

Increasing the number of sales representatives is an obvious option to achieve a higher level of sales, but achieving an optimal number of sales representatives is difficult. A number of software programmes can help the planner evaluate the return on investment, but there are also a number of manual systems. One of the most useful is to consider the return on time invested.

$$\text{ROTI (return on time invested)} = \frac{\text{gross margin on sales obtained}}{\text{cost of time invested}}$$

By calculating the potential sales base, the likely sales volume per call, and the average cost of the sales representatives' time (based on existing company data developed in Chapter 4), it is possible to identify, graphically, the likely optimum for sales force investment.

■ Increasing investment in identifying and developing new distribution channels

The company can sell more of the current product by identifying and exploiting new distribution channels along the lines of the discussion in Chapter 4. This will tend to be more expensive than either changes in sales management or improvements in quality control. The expanded customer base and greater level of activity will mean that the company will also have to devote more emphasis to credit control, with more credit checking, perhaps more staff and more sophisticated systems.

■ Increasing investment in logistics

With more stock, alternative or secondary warehouses may be needed to provide a higher level of service to certain parts of the operating area, which, of course, will require additional investment. Other logistical investments may involve more delivery vehicles.

■ Increasing investment in sales and media promotion

Defining the exact level of expenditure to achieve optimum returns is complicated, even for the most sophisticated companies. Where a company relies on direct response advertising – as the SME should – the returns from advertising can be quantified in that a certain level of investment should yield a certain level of return. Greater levels of investment will yield greater returns, up to an optimum level. This can be calculated simply using the equation:

Optimal lead generation = cross-over point where cost per existing lead + cost per additional lead is minimal.

With the greater expenditure on media promotion required by a market penetration policy, the use of a specialist advertising agency is likely to be a more viable option than in-house expertise. As with commissioning market research, specific and detailed advertising planning is required. This should include customers' buying criteria, the number of customers, objectives of the campaign, major competitive products, advantages of company product over competition, sales seasonality, sales targets, promotional budget, methods for measuring effectiveness, reporting system and reporting frequency.

■ Administrative issues

With the higher levels of activity involved in implementing a market penetration strategy, various administrative issues are bound to arise and the cost implications need to be evaluated. In addition to new discussion, the personnel and production systems fine-tuned in Chapter 4 need to be developed further.

- **Staff requirements/systems** The company is likely to need more people, either at the manual worker level or as supervisors and manager or specialists. A common issue in all expansion strategies, the planner will have to analyse personnel requirements by function by working back from the sales plan. Improvements will be needed in recruitment, appraisal and disciplinary systems, and in approaches to motivation. The costs of improving the flow of information within the company must also be considered.
- **Structure** A market penetration policy will rarely require a substantial alteration in company structure, although increased staff

numbers may mean more managers. Layers of supervisory staff should be minimised, so that the company keeps close to its customers and its staff.

- **Skills**   A market penetration policy is one that builds on existing skills. However, greater volumes mean production planning skills become more important, requiring investment in training.

- **Shared values/management style**   A rise in staff numbers may dilute the common values of the organisation. Additional action – information, quality circles (Chapter 4) and so on – may be needed to ensure that company values are strengthened. Management style may also become more autocratic as a larger number of customers must be serviced on time (Table 4.8).

- **Production or service supply implications**   More goods or services means more machines are required, which are probably of greater sophistication and/or involve a higher level of maintenance. There are also space implications, which will further raise investment requirements. All this assumes that the efficiency improvements made by fine-tuning – better use of space, additional shifts – have already been maximised. Again, assuming the relevant fine-tuning ideas described in Chapter 4 have been considered, production planning will require more investment, often because of changing order size. New customers tend to place smaller orders than established clients, with the result that production runs will be shorter and overall costs higher, unless these orders are integrated into the existing production. Improved scheduling of raw materials, component supply, production and logistics will reduce the impact on the cash flow.

- **Suppliers**   The greater volume of production or service supply may put pressures on existing suppliers of raw materials and components. Sourcing additional supplies may not be on the most advantageous credit terms. Alternatively, ordering materials in a different pattern may improve credit/pricing conditions.

- **Legal**   As the company expands, there will be a greater need to formalise and record agreements such as employment contracts, trade marketing agreements, supplier agreements. Investment in professional advice will therefore probably increase as part of the market penetration policy.

■ Finance issues

- **Cash flow** Expanded production will mean that the cash flow may become negative as the company funds the greater level of activity.
- **Working capital requirements** As volumes increase, the company will need to finance more stock, more work in progress and a greater level of debtors.
- **Capital investment for additional equipment** There may be a requirement for additional investment for new equipment.

CASE STUDY ## Softawater, part XXII

As Softawater's market penetration strategy involves known customers and products, the company feels that the existing information system will be adequate for controlling the new operation.

To implement the strategy, Softawater is using a mixture of increased investment in the sales force, new distribution channels and increased sales promotion. More sales representatives are required to cover the broader market more effectively. The major new distribution outlets the company has identified include the growing sector of healthfood shops, which provide a huge expansion opportunity, and offering a small, trial filter system is the main method that will be relied on to establish Softawater's products in these new outlets.

The company is also reviewing the potential for a coupon to be included in its current product that will enable the customer to buy five filters at a substantial discount from the store, thereby improving repeat purchase levels. At its present stage of development, Softawater considers that the level of expenditure on media is low and that using a specialist agency would be inappropriate. Managers plan to hold initial discussions with local agencies to see what services they could provide.

The strategy has few significant implications for suppliers, distribution, inventory and warehousing. The company will continue to use its current physical distribution system and although there will be higher levels of inventory, the existing warehouse area is adequate to meet the new storage requirements. Suppliers will be able to meet any increased demand for raw materials and components.

The implications of this higher level of activity are largely unimportant to production and production capacity. Softawater can increase its production by 150 per cent by means of an additional shift – and ensuring full utilisation of the existing equipment during the day shift. The investment in maintenance will need to rise, but no additional capital investment in equipment will be required in the first year. However, increased expenditure will be needed in the second and third years of the implementation of the strategy. The higher volumes of filters being produced will mean that cash flow will become negative for three months, but the bank has indicated that further finance will be available to deal with this shortfall.

Personnel policies will require some attention – especially in recruitment and appraisal. Credit control systems will be overhauled, and new procedures put in place.

MARKET DEVELOPMENT

Market development is riskier and more resource intensive than market penetration. There are therefore even better arguments for a systematic approach.

■ Market identification

Selecting the appropriate markets is the first step in creating a market development strategy. Which are the most attractive markets for the company? These are ones that have the right combination of product or service, competitive and corporate factors. The greater the proposed investment, the more important competitive and corporate factors become (Table 6.3).

Risk has been integrated into the discussion from the very earliest planning exercise in Chapter 2. Each market has its associated levels of risk. These involve changes in currency, inflation, political, market growth, legislative and competitive structure of the market.

Table 6.3   Issues to analyse when considering a market development strategy

Product issues	Competitive issues	Corporate issues
Market size	Market share structure	Corporate laws
Market growth	Quality comparison	Labour laws
Market profitability	Price position	Planning laws
Price elasticity	Distribution channel structure	Foreign exchange control
Market access	Logistics	Labour skills
Product laws	Promotional channels	Taxation, government support
Patents/copyrights/ trademarks	Promotional expenditure	Finance
	Suppliers	Business style
	Substitutes	Communication

■ Method of market entry

The business planner must next decide on the best compromise between market attractiveness, risk and investment for the chosen market. For the large corporation, there is a whole range of options. For the SME, the most practical investment route is to focus on a single international market, or a group of markets with common boundaries, and use a simple, low-cost, but flexible, method of entering the market.

For the SME, the most practical investment route is to focus on a single international market, or a group of markets with common boundaries, and use a simple, low-cost, but flexible, method of entering the market.

The main options, together with their advantages and disadvantages and a general view on risk and potential likely return, are in Table 6.4.

Table 6.4 The main options for market entry

Options	Advantages	Disadvantages	Potential risk	Potential return
Export wholesaler	Payment in own currency, organises shipment	Limited control over destination, poor pricing, limited sales, demand fluctuation	Low	Low
Overseas store group buying office	Payment in own currency, may organise shipment	Margins, control over development, contractual requirements, demand fluctuation	Low	Low
Agent	Direct contact with overseas customer	Credit risk, currency risk, many customers/ products, demand fluctuation, limited market knowledge	Low/ moderate	Low/ moderate
Distributor	Direct contact with customer, market coverage, marketing input, development potential	Currency risk, contractual problems, different sales agenda, promotional investment	Moderate	Moderate
Franchise	Market coverage, marketing input	Contractual problems, quality control, promotional investment	Moderate	Moderate
Direct sales from home office	Market coverage, pricing, marketing input	Customer service, promotional control	Moderate	Moderate/ high
Overseas sales office	Market coverage, market research	Cost, control	Moderate/ high	Moderate/ high
Local manufacture via third party and sales office	Product development, avoids currency exposure	Stockholding, finance, quality control, cost of developing distribution	High	High
Joint venture	Access to distribution network, additional finance to exploit market	Control, creation of potential competitor, resource implications	High	Moderate
Complete overseas facility	Product development, full access to market, develop local skills	Cost, competitive position, control	Very high	Very high

■ Quality control

New markets often mean higher quality, especially as the higher relative prices in the new markets demand it. Greater investment in quality control therefore becomes essential to implement market development policies effectively.

■ Sales management

The operation and management of the sales force will differ considerably from the home market. The new skills required may include one or more languages, negotiating techniques, training and market research, depending on customer type. The new sales team will tend to be more senior to the existing national sales force, giving rise to problems of integration, as well as motivating and managing a new, combined sales force.

■ Distribution, inventory and warehousing

Different markets often have different distribution channels with different servicing costs to those operating at home. Evaluating, developing and managing these channels is important to the effective implementation of a market development strategy. Increases or decreases in the costs of servicing a particular channel have to be identified and incorporated into the implementation plan.

Different markets may also demand different distribution methods. For the SME, the greatest change is likely to be a move towards unitised or containerised despatch to more distant markets. This may have implications for inventory management, packaging and warehouses' handling systems. In addition to ordering products in different quantities, new market development customers may require higher service levels, reorder times will change, alterations in patterns of demand may affect levels of safety stock and this also affects warehouse requirements.

There will be a series of trade-offs between customers' inventory requirements, the physical distribution system and warehouse costs. Nevertheless, the distance from the market is likely to involve the development of new warehousing. Also, customer trial involving an increase in the number of small orders, adds to the amount of work for the warehouse.

■ Order processing

Order processing becomes more complicated in many cases, with faraway markets wanting new and specific types of documentation. Where payment is a problem, an understanding of how documentary credits (letters of credit) function becomes essential to order processing, substantially increasing cost. Credit control also becomes an integral component. The potential for increases in small orders as a result of customer trial must also be considered.

■ Sales and/or media promotion

Techniques that work at home may not be appropriate in new markets. New approaches are needed to take account of legislation, customer requirements and the problems of administering sales promotion at a distance. Often this means concentrating on those techniques that are the simplest to operate and administer. In the early days of market development, sales promotion also needs to concentrate on trial, rather than repeat purchase.

A market development policy involves a greater investment in media promotion, the emphasis of the message being put on customers trialling the product. Where media promotion is part of the proposed action, it must be planned carefully to ensure that the message, promotional channel, frequency of advertisement and so on are appropriate for the market.

■ Price

A market development strategy also involves the SME planner in taking account of a completely different market with different price structures and quality perceptions. Pricing policy decisions must include the higher costs of servicing the market, and the implications of pricing in the local currency. In practical terms, most SMEs will have to choose a premium price position in the majority of markets – otherwise profitability would be severely reduced.

■ Administration issues

- **Structure, staff and skills** Businesses have to continually re-adjust their structures as the market development strategy becomes more successful. Initially, the export department reports to one particular division – perhaps sales and marketing – but, at some stage (usually when they are developing non-standard products), a separate department is needed. Where there is direct company investment in the overseas market, a separate corporate structure reporting to the main board of the parent company is normally required. Further development of the product, market and customers means further reorganisation is required, into a structure that coordinates the product of service and market – a matrix management system.

  Staff issues will be similar to those encountered in the market penetration strategy, but because market development is continuous, skills improvement for market development will mean significant investment in training and recruitment.

- **Shared values and management style** Market development makes a company more diverse and so maintaining corporate cohesion requires greater investment of time and planning.

  The type of management style required depends on the exact form the strategy takes. However, because of the distance between the head office and the customer, rules are more important to managing parts of the operation, emphasising a bureaucratic management style (see Table 4.8). This said, the evolutionary nature of the strategy means that many, and more complicated, problems – from customers, regulations and marketing – develop and these need to be resolved. This favours a more democratic management style.

- **Systems** With greater staff diversity in a more complicated, evolving organisation, more attention must be given to recruitment, appraisal, discipline and motivation to maintain effective corporate development. Greater emphasis also has to be given to internal communication.

- **Production**   Most of the production or service supply issues are likely to be similar to the problems posed by market penetration, though, as the company expands its presence in the overseas market, the demand for local variety becomes a more and more important issue in the medium term – leading on to new product development requirements.

- **Legal**   It is very important to document agreements for international development so that both sides are clear about the expectations. This often involves substantial investment in professional help. For example, a franchise agreement can run to 100, very detailed pages! Companies also need to ensure that appropriate legal protection for their copyrights, patents, or trademarks is available internationally before they commit to a market development policy. Where the creation of a subsidiary is involved, the legal ramifications may be considerable.

■ Financial issues

- **Cash flow**   Market development is likely to mean longer delivery periods, potentially lower margins on the initial orders (high costs of delivery, promotion, travel, sales force, combined with low volumes) and greater inventory requirements. All are likely to affect cash flow in the early part of implementation.

- **Profit and loss**   During the early stages, higher costs and lower margins will probably lower earnings. Profit and loss may also be influenced by currency translations and the management of costs between the parent and local company where there are overseas subsidiaries. Taxation becomes more complicated as a result – many companies are able to benefit from improved taxation planning.

- **Financial ratios**   Working capital needs to increase to fund the increased level of debtors, and, with the extended credit period often needed to service distant markets, the working capital ratio tends to worsen, as does debtor length.

Brainstorm, part XIV

Brainstorm has made an initial analysis of market attractiveness and a risk assessment, which suggested that the most attractive, lowest risk market is Eire. Expenditure on education is growing more rapidly in Eire than in the remainder of the European Union – the market is fragmented. The service Brainstorm provides is of a higher quality than that of local competitors. The market is profitable, with low price elasticity, and Brainstorm's price position is not significantly higher than that of the competition. The company can find reasonable quality staff, there are no problems with business style or communication, no taxation or foreign exchange issues that give cause for concern. Trademark protection can also be obtained easily.

To control Brainstorm's market development strategy, more detailed information on suppliers, revenues and costs is required. Certain cost centres would become a much more important factor when the company expands into new market areas. Brainstorm also has to spend considerably more on training and personnel development to aid implementation of the strategy.

Physical distribution has to change – the company has to establish a new warehouse system, involving higher levels of inventory. Order processing becomes no more complicated, although the volume of orders increases. Sales promotion techniques have to concentrate on trial initially, and the company has to invest more heavily in media promotion to draw the attention of the new customers to the product and service range being offered. There are many opportunities to take advantage of low-cost public relations, and cost-effective local newspapers and specialist magazines provide other media opportunities.

Brainstorm can charge a premium for its products in the new market because higher prices are expected and, therefore, profitability is not significantly damaged by this move. The taxation implications of the new market mean that it is more appropriate to take profit in the home market. The potential risk of significant currency fluctuations are not likely to have a serious impact on overall profitability.

NEW PRODUCT OR SERVICE DEVELOPMENT

Turning an idea into a successful, profitable product or service is not just luck. It requires careful evaluation of opportunities and risks.

■ Marketing issues

Product or service development strategies involve marketing in two separate stages. The first concerns making decisions about what products to develop – a process of product definition, culminating in the creation of a protocol that defines, in detail, what the product or service should be. The second is the development of the marketing plan, or a phase of commercialisation, which includes testing and market introduction.

▓ *Market definition*

- **Product or service development themes**   As with market development, and for highly practical reasons, the SME planner should select from a narrow range of options when deciding which products to develop. The more attractive the market, and the stronger the position of the SME within that market, the greater the level of investment that should be considered. (Table 6.5, reading it in conjunction with Table 5.11, page 138.)
- **Information collection**   Identifying market opportunities from the wide range of alternative sources of information is obviously important to the product or service development process.
- **Protocol development**   The protocol describes exactly what the new product's or service's benefits should be – size, weight, colour, performance, durability, packaging, technical support, availability and price.

▓ *Commercialisation*

- **Testing**   It is essential to test the product or service, prior to its full-scale launch, to check that the initial research and the protocol were accurate, that the specification defined by the market is still wanted, and that the total package is as close to what the customers want as possible. Testing will also enable the company to

Table 6.5   Issues in new product or service development

Categories of new products or services	Market attractiveness	Company structure – best option	Investment
Sector creating – technical	Major product innovations that open new markets	'Academic' – close liaison between research and production	High, not for SMEs
Performance enhancement – technical	'Better mousetraps' generally for brand leaders; new product's 'edge' important	'Rugby scrum' – clear goals, speed, liaison between development and production	Lower than above but still high
Technological reorganisation – technical	Allows rapid market penetration, if successful	'Rugby scrum'	Lower than above
Process – technical, new production capacity	For mature industries – competitive advantage from improved production	'Rugby scrum'	High
Reformulation – technical and marketing	For market penetration	'Coffee shop' – close customer contact, production and customer liaison	Route for SMEs
Branding – marketing	Builds consumer franchise	'Coffee shop'; marketing and advertising liaison	High
Service – marketing	Competitive edge, rapid growth	'Coffee shop'	Possible for SMEs
Design – technical and marketing	Competitive edge for products modified for markets	'Coffee shop'	Good for SMEs
Packaging – marketing, technical	Improved product performance, changes buying behaviour	'Coffee shop'	Good for SMEs

(Use in conjunction with Table 5.11)

fine-tune the production and identify whether or not the initial volume and revenue projections are accurate, while also fine-tuning the marketing support programme.

- **Sales management**   Often, new products or services mean new skills and new knowledge. The customer must be introduced to new products or concepts, which means longer and more sales calls to cover the customer base during the launch. Therefore, for selling, the investment implications of new product development are considerable.

- **Logistical issues**   Ensuring that the new product meets distribution channels' requirements will be part of the initial protocol development. There may be distinct variations between the different channels' attitudes to a new product or service – some may prefer to stick with the old.

  As with market development, order processing may experience a substantial increase in the number of small orders as customers try the new product or service. New products increase inventory, unless the new product is entirely replacing the old. Safety stock levels for new products need to be set high in readiness for the early stage of commercialisation.

  New products needing new handling methods require further investment, and when the overall volumes sold are rising, work in the warehouse also grows – especially if there is a large number of small orders.

- **Sales and/or media promotion**   Many models of the eventual success of a new product or service suggest that the rate of trial early in its introduction determines the eventual level of market sale. Increased investment in both sales and media promotion is crucial to achieving trial. For new products or services, a complete analysis of the structure of the campaign is necessary to evaluate the effectiveness of the chosen promotion channels, what the message should be, the frequency with which that message should be broadcast and the inclusion of response material. Again, the initial emphasis must be on trial – a clear explanation of why the product or service is superior to the competition's, who should try it and what the benefits are.

- **Price**   Pricing a new product or service is one of the most difficult parts of planning. It must be based on a realistic assessment of the current market pricing levels and the competitive advantages of the new product. A totally new product or service, with no reference point, is even more difficult to price. Detailed testing resolves many of the pricing problems associated with introducing new items into established markets, and new items into new market categories.

■ Administration

■ **Structures, systems and staffing** The new product or service development option chosen has a profound effect on the structure of the company, so any plan must take account of this. Table 6.5 lists a number of approaches to new product development and the company approach best suited to each (see also Table 5.11). Other structural changes for effective product development must involve a clear reporting structure within the firm, with a single director responsible for the project, a well-defined project team with responsibility and authority. As new product development is labour-intensive, companies should also plan to allow the staff involved to give it their full attention. This is often when subcontracting or interim management is an extremely viable option.

The product or service development decision also affects requirements for special skills. The SME's management has to be prepared to either develop these in-house by detailed training or via recruitment. In turn, this has impacts on other aspects of staffing. Changes to recruitment, appraisal and motivational components may have to be considered. Improvements in internal communication become important because of changes in the organisation. With a range of diverse and new activities, often involving the cooperation of staff from different departments, making sure that all individuals are aware of the importance and relevance of the new product development to the future of the company is a vital part of company systems development.

■ **Management style and shared values** Management style, to a large extent, depends on the time constraints of the project and the type of product or service development involved (Tables 4.12 and 6.5). More time and effort have to be given by management to ensure that the diverse groups within the organisation are working effectively towards a common goal.

■ **Production and production efficiencies** New products or services may mean investment in new equipment or a combination of additional new equipment and more of the existing equipment. New equipment may need new skills and so an investment in training. These skills may also take time to develop, affecting profits because the more units of a single product a company produces, the lower the unit cost. Often called the learning or experience curve, organisations improve their performance as a task is repeated. Given all these factors, initial production runs of a new product are unlikely to meet the efficiencies of existing products that have been manufactured for a long period.

Additional equipment has an impact on space requirements and may significantly affect the flow of work within the unit. The workplace layout must receive attention to ensure that the new product line does not reduce productivity.

- **Quality control**   Investment in testing equipment, training and development of effective quality systems should precede the introduction of a new product or service as it is essential that the product is of the highest possible quality.
- **Suppliers**   New products or services may also mean new raw materials, and new components, which may not be available from existing suppliers.
- **Legal**   New products or services may mean a considerable increase in documentation. The product or service could be either patentable or subject to copyright, design or trademark protection. All of these options require considerable work to ensure that the commercial property in which the company has invested is as secure as possible.

■ Financial issues

- **Cash flow**   Accurate planning for new product development projects needs to be incorporated into the cash flow and include extra staff costs, production development costs, equipment costs, testing, training and commercialisation.
- **Profit and loss**   Product development has substantial effects on profitability – by raising costs – and this needs to be taken into account in the business plan.
- **Balance sheet**   For the typical SME, the issue of how to value intellectual property or research and development is of little interest. These are issues for some companies to explore with their professional advisers.

Softawater, part XXIII

A major redirection and reorganisation is necessary for product development to be effective within Softawater.

First, the company clarifies the type of innovation it should be focusing
on. It is clear that much of the earlier effort has been ill advised and that the
company should be concentrating instead on technological reorganisation
for the consumer division, and in the weaker industrial division on service
(Tables 5.11 and 6.5). The choice of these two routes clarifies what type of
organisational structure should be chosen for each division – separating
the product development teams, a problem the company had not earlier
considered to be important. The consumer division team is to focus on performance enhancement and the delivery of clear specifications (rugby
scrum), while the industrial team needs to modify processes via close contact with the customer (a coffee shop approach; see Table 6.5).

Within the company, clear reporting structures are to be created, with a
single board member being entirely responsible for the day-to-day decisions. The entire board is to be involved in presentations of key milestones.

Its choice of the innovation route determines where the team should
source its information concerning possible new developments. It also
means that the team leader and team structure can be decided on – the
team leader for the consumer project needs to be an individual with production management skills, while, in the industrial division, the emphasis
has to be on marketing and customer analysis.

Both of the projects are to be managed with the use of standard industry software, the plans being broken down into tasks, activities and milestones. The customer project is to initially start from the development of a
protocol after the analysis of market potential. The team has discovered
that a major gap exists in the market for a consumer product, packed in a
clear plastic cone, that changes colour when the filter system is no longer
effective. The technology for this innovation is available from the oil industry, which uses a similar system to determine the effectiveness of its water
recycling systems.

The protocol describes the exact requirements for the product, derived
from the analysis of the market – the price, product performance and when
the item should become available. The product specification fits the current physical dimensions of the existing filter range. The external surface
is to be made of the same thickness of plastic as the existing product, but

the plastic used is to be clear rather than opaque. The resinous granules are to be initially blue and change to red when the effectiveness of the resin is exhausted. The performance of the resin needs to match or improve on existing efficiencies, and be entirely non-toxic. Market research indicates that consumers are prepared to pay an additional 7 per cent to know when the filter is exhausted.

From this protocol, the team can work out the investment requirements of the project, divided into those for production, and marketing and sales. The production issues that are considered to be important are:

- raw materials and components' requirements;
- supplier availability;
- production systems, capacity and costs;
- new equipment requirements;
- skills of production personnel;
- training requirements;
- production efficiencies over time.

Softawater has to use new suppliers, although existing production equipment can still be used, and the likely sales level is not going to cause capacity problems; there is no need for new equipment investment in the short term. As the new product can be handled in the same way as the existing range, production skills are adequate, so there is no need for training. Also, the introduction of the new product does not require a learning period as volumes and expertise are built up.

The marketing issues are:

- testing procedures;
- customers;
- sales promotion requirement;
- media requirement;
- sales force numbers, skills, training;
- physical distribution;
- inventory – new product;
- inventory – existing product;
- warehousing;
- order processing.

Softawater has already developed a customer panel that provides an accurate cross-section of the company's customer base because of previous new product tests. Each of the stores is happy to provide the company with detailed information about the speed of sales compared with the existing product range.

The company is targeting the existing customer base. Demonstration units for the new system can be developed from the existing trial product without major modification, although the numbers needed are far greater. As the company thinks it has a major market opportunity, it is intending to invest more heavily in coupon offers to encourage trial. Direct mail in certain key areas is also a potentially profitable promotion route.

Softawater can use the same physical distribution methods as it does for its existing product range. Inventory levels of the new product range can be worked back from projections within the marketing plan, but an unknown quantity is the overall effect on the existing product range. Softawater is quite happy if the entire volume of the existing range is replaced by the new, as it is substantially more profitable. The higher levels of inventory are not going to affect warehousing requirements, nor have much impact on order processing.

With the similarity of the product and its demands on production there would be limited impact on the organisation. The main implications for financial planning would be on cash flow. The project plan, converted into investment requirements, means a substantial outflow for the initial six months, followed by significant returns. The overall effect on the profit and loss account would be to reduce profitability in the early part of the year, but enhance it over the full year.

By contrast, the industrial product development is likely to make significant demands on the entire organisation, throughout sales, promotion and service support.

DIVERSIFICATION

A diversification strategy is the route carrying the highest risk for all businesses (Chapter 5, Table 5.16). For the SME, the demands of diversification on finance, management skills and production capacity make it unrealistic unless:

- the company has a major problem with seasonal cash flow, and the introduction of new activities would significantly smooth this;
- the company faces a disappearing market, either as a result of changing patterns of demand or regulatory pressures.

In such circumstances, the company should attempt to develop products or services that:

- involve the same production systems and/or sales skills;
- use the same distribution system.

IMPLEMENTATION ROUTES

For most SMEs, strategic development is an organic process – depending on the availability of internal resources to exploit the market opportunity. Naturally, other options exist – the company can achieve its strategic objectives via acquisition or a joint venture. Where these alternatives are being considered, a comparison between organic development and the other route(s) needs to be made.

■ Acquisition

Acquisition is often a very tempting route, promising rapid growth, new customers, new products and new expertise. The other side is that the acquirer takes on a whole range of liabilities, for which it may have to pay a considerable sum of money, and a whole range of problems over which it may not have adequate control (often called 'elephant traps').

■ Due diligence

Being systematic about acquisition is vital, both before the due diligence process and afterwards – post-acquisition management. Due diligence should answer all of the following questions.

- Is the acquirer gaining a stable customer base?
- Is the acquirer gaining a declining product range or one with substantial potential?
- Is the acquirer likely to face problems with the suppliers of raw materials or components?
- Are there serious financial liabilities that the acquirer will face?

- Are there serious political or public relations issues that the acquirer will face?
- Will the acquirer have to invest heavily in production equipment and training to bring the target company up to the necessary standard?
- What effect will the target company have on company earnings in the short, medium and long term?
- Will the acquirer be able to retain the key staff members after the acquisition?
- Can the information system be effectively integrated into the parent company's without major investment?

Each of these issues requires judgements from management about the importance of the factor and how many problems the existing and future position are likely to cause, and to build in safeguards as part of the acquisition documentation, creating warranties and guarantees wherever possible.

▓ Characteristics of successful acquisitions

Studies suggest, not surprisingly, that the most successful acquisitions are those made by companies that approach them with the aim of adding to their existing operations, rather than subtracting from them. The acquisition can be seen as complementary, and the tendency in these successful takeovers is for the chosen company to not be too culturally distinct in management style from the acquirer's own.

Companies that manage takeovers well are also extremely systematic. They analyse their target company in detail and have a clearly defined plan as to how they will integrate the target company once the acquisition is completed. They also have a clear price that they are prepared to pay for the business.

▓ Post-acquisition management

A post-acquisition plan that allocates responsibilities for what should be done over time is crucial. The exact structure of such a plan will depend on the type and complexity of the target firm, but an outline of possible activities is given in Table 6.6.

Table 6.6   A post-acquisition plan of action

Day 1	Month 1	Month 3	Month 12
Reviews of: ■ liabilities; ■ customers: sales and order book, sales plan, distribution; ■ products/ services, quality control; ■ equipment/ maintenance; ■ purchasing, suppliers; ■ information systems' integration with acquirer's; ■ health and safety. Start environ-mental audit.	Reviews of: ■ staff skills, training; ■ staff contracts, job des-criptions; ■ staff pay and conditions; ■ inventory and stock; ■ facilities management; ■ R&D efficiency; ■ operations. Decide on: ■ sub-contracting. Identify: ■ supplier alternatives; ■ benchmark companies. Complete: ■ vendor ranking.	Reviews of: ■ skills; ■ management/ supervisory performance; ■ cost centres; ■ production and speed of service; ■ product range. Complete: appraisal of managers and supervisors.	Reviews of: ■ benchmarks; ■ health and safety; ■ skills. Environmental audit.

■ Joint venture

A joint venture, by contrast, is a far less common route for business development. This option is, in practical terms for the SME, limited to those markets that cannot, for legal reasons, be exploited by a wholly owned subsidiary or operating unit.

A joint venture must be carefully planned and monitored. Experi-ence suggests a number of key problem areas. Some of these are strategic – for example, the transfer of technical knowledge from one partner to another means the creation of a potential competitor. The different priorities and management styles of the partners can make it difficult to implement particular strategies or policies, often simply because of poor communication.

Again, joint ventures work where a systematic approach is used. For example, where the joint venture is established for a limited and specific period and the supplier of the technology clearly defines what technology will – or will not – be available. In these cases, key technology will be provided in component form.

CASE
STUDY ## Brainstorm, part XV

One option before Brainstorm for its proposed market development in Eire is the acquisition of Daley, a small chain of toy shops with three outlets in the main towns. Educational products make up about 40 per cent of the group's sales, with the rest being accounted for by toys for the under-ten age group. Brainstorm would acquire a stable customer base (the chain has been selling toys for 30 years), the potential is considerable, there are few problems with suppliers, it appears that there are few major liabilities and no political or public relations problems. New staff would need training to improve their knowledge of the product range and the educational applications of the toys.

The costs of the acquisition could be met from the large cash balances of Brainstorm, and forecasts suggest that the three new stores are likely to be more profitable than the existing outlets, improving overall profitability and earnings. There is no problem in keeping existing staff, although the directors of Brainstorm feel that a policy of gradual replacement with younger staff could improve the effectiveness of the entire operation.

The current information system is a manual process that could easily be replaced with Brainstorm's own, although the directors feel that an investment in improved information management would yield benefits for the entire group.

SUMMARY

This chapter has taken the general concept of strategy and analysed its detailed impact on each part of the SME, identifying where the costs are likely to fall and what changes need to be made in each functional area.

It has stressed that each strategy makes different and distinct demands on the organisation, which must be prepared to make not just the necessary investment, but also accept that other issues will affect the success of the implementation of the chosen strategy.

The plan in detail

INTRODUCTION

So far, the current state of the SME, how its performance could be improved and the implications of strategic alternatives in order to decide where it should be going have been examined. The building up of the final plan is therefore a combination of what is happening with the existing business, and what has been decided for the new year. The route taken is always to build up from the customer, rather than down from the company.

> The SME is always restricted by a shortage of cash, and concentrating on cash flow ensures that the company will survive by managing its relationships with its financial supporters, customers and suppliers.

Cash is king. The SME is always restricted by a shortage of cash, and concentrating on cash flow ensures that the company will survive by managing its relationships with its financial supporters, customers and suppliers. Every business must use the information system already established as part of the business plan – starting with the cash flow, moving on to the profit and loss and balance sheet, and then a consideration of the control implications for financial ratios, production, personnel and marketing.

STEP 1: SET FIXED COSTS

Identify items that remain in the fixed cost environment from the previous year.

The most practical approach is to start with the existing cash flow and identify those components that will remain fixed for the following year.

CASE STUDY **Softawater, part XXIV**

For the chosen market penetration strategy, Softawater does not see that its costs for premises, travel, professional services or equipment will all rise irrespective of the overall level of sales. A similar view is taken regarding the level of miscellaneous costs.

STEP 2: SET BASE VOLUMES

Establish the maintenance – or base – volumes and related costs. Identify continuing business by volume, broken down by customer, area and product.

The creation of trade marketing agreements with major customers (see Chapter 4, Table 4.7) greatly simplifies the planning process by reducing the level of uncertainty. Where trade marketing agreements do not exist, the careful planner includes the level of existing business as the baseline, regardless of the fact that the market may be growing, as an initial, conservative estimate of what sales volumes will be in the next planning period.

When an information system developed in this way is finished, the SME is able to generate a complete analysis by customer and area to define profitability by both. Once the SME reaches a certain size, it is likely to need a system of account management in which each major customer is treated as a profit centre, with all the relevant service costs for that customer identified separately.

Within this breakdown, existing relationships between products and cost centres can be included – sales calls, cost per call, deliveries, cost per delivery, inventory cost per unit, warehousing cost per unit, sales promotion by customer or by product, and any media promotion that is customer- or area-related. Costs can also be introduced of raw materials and components, using suppliers' forecasts of raw material movements and any possible contract on the supply of components or subcontracting work, and company estimates of the effects of improving productivity and overall production.

The fixed labour component of all of these products can also be included from the standard production time calculation, on a unit-by-unit basis. A calculation can also be included from production costing of the total utility cost per unit of production, based on the forecast of inflation in pay for the next year – or, where companies have plant-wide agreements, the impact of these on production costs (see Table 7.1).

Table 7.1   Maintenance relationships between products and cost centres

Factor	Product A	B	C	Customer A	B	C	Area A	B	C
Volume									
Deliveries									
Cost per delivery									
Sales calls									
Cost per call									
Sales promotion									
Inventory									
Order numbers									
Order cost per unit									
Warehouse cost per unit									
Raw materials									
Subcontract									
Pay – production									
Utilities									

CASE STUDY   **Brainstorm XVI**

With its stable customer base, Brainstorm can rapidly calculate the new position for the following year. The directors have decided not to include market growth at this stage of the calculation, although, with demand growing at 8 per cent for the next year, the initial planned volumes are conservative.

The main suppliers are all able to provide the company with firm prices for the year. Many of the other costs are fixed, rather than varying with turnover, although the number of orders per employee will need to be carefully watched as the firm is already finding it difficult to service the customer base at peak periods, even with extra staff.

STEP 3: SET PRICES

Set prices, discount levels and credit for all existing business. Pricing remains an art rather than an exact science, but the aim is to achieve the maximum revenue for the firm. In order to do this, the following have to be assessed:

- the likely movements in average market price;
- the competitive position of the company;
- the impact of quality improvements on price;
- the rate of market growth, price elasticity and its effect on the price/volume relationship;
- the effects of promotional investment.

Say that an existing average market price is 100. The inflation trends in the market suggest that for that market, and that market alone (remember, each market sector has a different rate of inflation), next year the average price will be 103.

In that market, the company's price position has been 80 over the past year. This suggests that the market price should be 82.4 for the next year, if competitive pressures are not going to increase.

However, the company has improved its quality significantly in the past year and, based on experience of the quality and price relationships in that particular market (remember, quality and price relationships vary from sector to sector), feels it can increase its prices by 3 per cent. This now establishes the market price as 84.8, to achieve the same percentage market share as last year.

The market is growing at 5 per cent. This means that, at 84.8, the company should sell 5 per cent more products or services than in the previous year. The market in which the firm operates has a price elasticity of 3 – that is, that a 1 per cent movement in relative price will mean a 3 per cent drop in sales. Such an elasticity would enable the company to increase its price to 86.2 without reducing the total volume of sales, while significantly enhancing profitability, providing that the relationship between revenue and costs remains the same. The use of the marginal profitability model in Chapter 4, under Fine-tuning sales, can help here.

Finally, promotional investment can also influence the price position. For the SME in the above example, investment in promotion is limited and is not enough to influence the pricing position.

The price range is further complicated by a company's discount and credit system. Reducing the level of discount will obviously have a major effect on the net prices achieved, but the impact of alterations on credit policy will be no less real, based on a finance cost of 1 per cent every 30 days.

The problems pricing pose become even more acute for a new product or service. When a new product is similar to those already in the company's or a competitor's range, a similar exercise to that for existing products can be carried out. However, when the product or service is significantly different from those currently available, the only potential source of pricing information will be detailed research on the acceptability of the new product or service (see Chapter 6, under New product or service development, Marketing issues, organisational and financial implications of selected strategies).

Once decisions on the pricing level have been taken, the planning team should discuss their acceptability with as many individuals as possible, both internally and externally. Severe price resistance from customers often means that the planned pricing level will have to be changed or discounts or credit altered.

CASE STUDY Softawater, part XXV

The inflation trends in the water softener market are for there to be an increase of 1 per cent over the previous year. Softawater's existing weighted market average price is 95 per cent. On this basis, the company could increase its price to 96 to remain in line with the market.

The relative quality position had not changed, and the company cannot take advantage of an improved quality relationship. With the increase in the market size of 5 per cent per annum, an increase in price would be achieved, but in a market with a price elasticity of 5, the returns would not be substantial. As the company is planning to follow a market penetration policy, an increase in price is not considered appropriate, especially as the majority of customers are hostile to any increase above inflation. Both credit and discount terms are to remain unchanged with the major customers with which Softawater has negotiated trade marketing agreements.

STEP 4: MARKET PENETRATION ADJUSTMENTS

Add the market penetration volumes, values and investment necessary to achieve the target. Once the maintenance position of the business has been established, you can build on the existing base with the additional volumes that will be generated by the market penetration policy, together with the costs relating to the new business that is planned – sales callage increase, sales promotion increase, media promotion expenditure. As volumes increase, the overall cost of delivery and warehouse operation may decline. As the plan is built up, such implications will have to be studied as they arise.

Each of these layers on top of the original maintenance volumes has an impact on production labour costs, equipment costs and warehousing that have to be added in as you build up the plan (see Table 7.2).

Table 7.2   Planned relationships between products and cost centres

Factor	Product A	B	C	Customer A	B	C	Area A	B	C
Volume									
Deliveries									
Cost per delivery									
Sales calls									
Cost per call									
Sales promotion									
Media promotion									
Inventory									
Order numbers									
Order cost per unit									
Warehouse per unit									
Raw materials									
Subcontract									
Pay – production									
Utilities									

STEP 5: MARKET DEVELOPMENT ADJUSTMENTS

Add the market development volumes, values and necessary investment. SME planners must fully cost the problems of servicing the new market – the higher promotion costs, distribution costs, sales costs, order processing costs. Pricing will also need to reflect the entirely different market environment, and its requirements, such as conversion into local currency, the different levels of sales tax and so on.

CASE STUDY ### Brainstorm, part XVII

Brainstorm has decided to purchase the Daley chain to achieve its market development strategy in Eire. The costs of the purchase, the additional inventory the stores require to provide back-up warehousing in the local market – all require substantial investment. The directors have also decided that Brainstorm needs to invest substantially in media and sales promotion to achieve trial in the new areas in which it is attempting to become established. The pricing position of the company could be higher than in the home market, reflecting the higher market prices of products imported into the country. A higher level of sales tax means still higher prices.

STEP 6: NEW PRODUCT OR SERVICE DEVELOPMENT ADJUSTMENTS

Add the new product or service volumes/values and necessary investment. The new product or service development programme operates as a separate cost base, with the investment necessary to achieve the various stages of protocol development, testing and commercialisation. It is sensible to include all expenditure relating to new product of service development in one category, so that the cost centre can be more easily controlled.

Forecasting product or service volumes and prices requires detailed analysis. Often, new products are slower to establish themselves than expected because of problems with quality, production or achieving trial. Another complicated area is the impact on production or service supply. The impact on production efficiencies, new equipment requirements and training can significantly affect the overall operation of the production plant. This has to be allowed for when incorporating the new product plans into the complete analysis. All these areas have been examined in the process of building up the plan from Chapter 3 onwards.

STEP 7: ADD OTHER INCOME

Add any other income. Many companies are able to gain income from other sources, such as government grants for training, premises conversion, energy conservation and the like. Grants are provided by a variety of funding institutions, including:

- local government;
- development agencies;
- international funds (the EU, for example);
- government support.

Only when grants have been formally approved should they be added to the developing cash flow with any additional cost that may be involved. Some grants, for example, demand a 50 per cent contribution from the company.

STEP 8: OTHER COSTS

Add supervisory costs and additional investment (plant, training, professional services).

At this stage, the SME planner has a complete picture of what volumes of products are being sold to which customers, and their impact on workloads throughout the organisation. From the level of activity within the various parts of the company, a decision will have to be made as to whether the existing supervisory management is adequate, can be reduced in the medium term or needs to be increased.

STEP 9: REVENUE STREAMS

Convert volumes to seasonal patterns to produce the revenue stream, margins and cash flow. Most businesses are unrealistic about how long it will take for new business to become established. The business planner has

Most businesses are unrealistic about how long it will take for new business to become established. ... it is better to err on the conservative, rather than enthusiastic, side.

to use existing experience regarding the growth in volumes with existing customers, or at new sites, to model how volume will grow. Again it is better to err on the conservative, rather than enthusiastic, side.

STEP 10: FUNDING REQUIREMENTS

Consider the impact of the plan on funding requirements.

By now, the SME planner has a clear idea of how cash flows through the organisation, and whether or not this will pose problems with funding, both in the short and medium term. Funding institutions need to be advised of what the peak borrowing demands will be, well in advance, so that costs can be minimised. New finance also takes time to arrange.

At this stage, it is necessary to check the viability of the proposed investment(s) and compare the alternatives that may exist. There are various different methods for separating projects, the most valuable of which is net present value, which, again, concentrates on the cash flow implications of investment policies.

Net present value works on the basis that, for the same level of monetary return, short-term inflows are more valuable to a company than longer-term ones are. In other words, the effect of time is to discount the value of money. Net present value calculations are therefore based on an agreed discount rate, and the cash flows over time.

Net present value = initial investment + discounted value of revenue – discounted value of costs

Another advantage of net present value is that it is highly flexible. It can allow for different timings of investments, and different rates of return from different types of investment. For example, a company could look at the implications of building a small factory initially, and adding to it, or else of building a large plant initially or combine demand probabilities of such an exercise in a decision tree (*step 11*).

The payback period is also a useful measure for short-term financing, and is simply the measure of how quickly the entire investment is repaid out of earnings.

STEP 11: TIMING AND CASH FLOW

The financial impact of any strategy can be altered by changes in the timings of implementation. Moving the start date of the implementation will often be sufficient to smooth the finances and reduce peak demands, although changes in implementation dates may also influence the overall chances of success of the project.

The use of a decision tree may be helpful in understanding the planning requirements of various options that involve a choice of implementation routes, each with different timing implications.

The use of a decision tree may be helpful in understanding the planning requirements of various options that involve a choice of implementation routes, each with different timing implications. An example would be to choose whether or not to buy either low- or high-volume equipment, each with different costs. The return would then be determined by what happens to market demand in the years following. The business planner can give probabilities for each of the demand levels in years one and two and calculate the overall returns in both. Decision trees are flexible; they also allow the planner to consider whether additional investment is likely to be needed, under certain circumstances, and add this to the tree (see Figure 7.1).

High-volume production				Low-volume production			
Year 1: demand probability							
High demand 0.6		Low demand 0.4		High demand 0.6		Low demand 0.4	
Year 2: demand probability							
High 0.8	Low 0.2	High 0.4	Low 0.6	High 0.8	Low 0.2	High 0.6	Low 0.4
Year 2: levels of return							
1	5	2	7	3	6	4	8

Fig. 7.1   Decision tree in spreadsheet format

STEP 12: MEETING THE PLANNED OBJECTIVES

Evaluate the other objectives of the plan against the overall outcome of the first draft business plan against other objectives. Does it meet the general requirement for gross profit, new product development, fixed costs, skills levels? Does it mean too much risk, too rapid a rate of growth, potential loss of control?

At this point, there may need to be a considerable change of emphasis in the plan, with major changes being made to levels of activity and cost. In many other cases, the plan will be broadly acceptable, but will require fine-tuning to achieve the necessary targets. The first fine-tuning will be to consider the interaction of various parts of the plan with each other – the development of trade-offs.

STEP 13: TRADE-OFFS

Where changing the timing of various investments is still not sufficient to achieve the required result, the planner needs to consider possible trade-offs in the plan.

■ Alternatives to changing the price of a product or service

▓ *Manufacturing trade-offs*

Reduce raw material consumption by redesigning; improve quality control; reduce high-cost ingredients; reduce production waste by improving the quality of the ingredients; improve or change the subcontractor contribution; improve maintenance and/or operations such as storage and handling; improve manufacturing efficiency by investing in more cost-effective machinery; or improve the factory layout; reduce overheads by subletting unused space; reduce raw material stocks by implementing better ordering procedures; minimise overtime and maximise factory staff performance; introduce performance-related pay structures or employ more part-time staff; improve purchasing procedures by widening the range of competitive quotes, increasing order quantities or changing financing methods; reduce losses by improving security or stock control.

■ *Product trade-offs*

Reduce or increase the range; provide extended guarantee periods; increase or reduce credit.

■ *Distribution trade-offs*

Reduce stockholdings; reorganise warehouse systems; change the physical distribution methods; change the level of service offered, such as the frequency of delivery or size of the order; use new distribution channels.

■ *Pricing trade-offs*

Change the discounting system or structure; combine products across ranges to improve discounting.

■ *Promotional trade-offs*

Change sales force management to sell more profitable products; sell to more profitable customers; sell more effectively by training, by reorganising work loads; change promotional investment; better organisation of media expenditure; more memorable advertisements; switch media to sales promotion.

■ Alternatives to raising promotional expenditure

▓ *Product trade-offs*

Improve quality control; develop new uses for packaging materials; redesign packaging; improve display ability; improve guarantees.

▓ *Public relations trade-offs*

Investigate ways in which to use public relations more effectively.

▓ *Sales force trade-offs*

Increase the numbers; change selling techniques, as they have in, for example, telephone sales; train and support the sales force more effectively; reorganise the sales force.

▓ *Distribution trade-offs*

Increase the number of intermediaries; change the pricing structure to improve motivation.

▓ *Pricing trade-offs*

Reduce the price; provide improved credit.

■ Alternatives to changing the nature of the product

▓ *Manufacturing trade-offs*

Investigate improved manufacturing techniques; improve staff training.

▓ *Distribution trade-offs*

Develop new distribution channels; use more intermediaries; reduce the price; change the price structure to encourage distribution; combine products with others.

▓ *Promotional trade-offs*

Increase promotion to encourage purchase; change promotional methods; improve training of the sales force; change the emphasis of the activity; change your targeted customers; improve the service provided by the sales force.

■ Alternatives to increasing workforce numbers

▨ *Promotion trade-offs*

Use more end-user oriented promotional material; use more coupon or direct response material; provide improved point of sale or information brochures.

▨ *Distribution trade-offs*

Use more intermediaries; direct marketing; and use third parties for specific sales tasks.

▨ *Personnel trade-offs*

Train; change the recruitment policy; redefine jobs; use technology to make the workforce more effective.

Where trade-offs do not produce the required effect, the business planner may need to consider further reductions in cost, but the effect of this is a lowering of the level of service provided to each customer.

STEP 14: SERVICE LEVELS

The business planner can cut costs further by lowering the level of service provided to each customer. Planners need to be careful about making reductions in service from the level agreed as this is essential to achieving competitive advantage – further reductions may harm the SME's competitive positioning.

STEP 15: NEW TARGETS

Create new profit and loss, balance sheet, financial ratios, production efficiency targets, personnel efficiency targets, marketing efficiency targets and new product development targets.

This completes the planning cycle that was first introduced in Chapter 1 (see Figure 1.1), setting new goals, performance criteria that can be used to both monitor the performance of the business and create a new base against which future long-term development can be decided.

SUMMARY

This chapter has concentrated on the detailed building up of a business plan, starting with the existing business and, from there, adding the implications of all the various strategies as a layering process to complete a pro forma cash flow. The resulting cash flow, and the other items of management information, are then compared with the overall objectives, and a process of fine-tuning the plan is then completed, should the broad objectives be inconsistent with the outcome of the plan.

At the end of this exercise, the business planner has a new base point that can be used to update the information system, completing the loop introduced in Figure 1.1. The entire process of monitoring, evaluating, and identifying new opportunities can start again.

Action and contingency planning

INTRODUCTION

Once the plan is complete, the planner needs to review it critically. Remember the SURE mnemonic of Chapter 2. Is the plan soundly based, do we understand the issues, is it realistic, have we put experienced people into areas of responsibility to complete the plan?

The next four stages described in this chapter fine-tune the plan and attempt to make it doubly SURE, if at all possible. These four stages are:

- listing the key assumptions that are part of the plan;
- measuring the effects significant changes will have on the plan via a sensitivity analysis;
- the creation of a contingency plan;
- a schedule of responsibilities and dates that contribute to an action plan.

ASSUMPTIONS

Often one of the most difficult areas of business planning is that of ensuring that the correct assumptions have been included in the plan. This is because many of the assumptions made in a business plan are never explicitly stated – the planner takes them to be factors of the environment that are so well established they are not worth discussing. However, checking through an established list is the only way to ensure that all issues are properly assessed (see Table 8.1).

Many of the assumptions made in a business plan are never explicitly stated – the planner takes them to be factors of the environment that are so well established they are not worth discussing. However, checking through an established list is the only way to ensure that all issues are properly assessed.

Another useful addition to the assessment of assumptions is to identify the level of risk associated with each. High-risk assumptions need additional consideration in two respects. First, whether additional investment in information might reduce the risk of a particular assumption. Second, it is necessary to underline the importance of a contingency plan to deal with problems that may arise should the assumption prove to be incorrect.

Table 8.1 Checklist for assessing assumptions

Area	Issue	Importance	Risk
Legislation – international			
Legislation – national			
Legislation – local			
Economic growth			
Inflation			
Disposable income change			
Social change			
Technology			
Competitive structure			
Competitive activity			
Competitive response to strategy			
Product quality			
Customer stability			
Production capacity			
Staff availability			
Finance availability			

SENSITIVITY ANALYSIS

The plan has been built up on the basis of a realistic assessment of sales and costs. Part of the review system should include an assessment of what the implications of significant variations from the expected outcomes – if sales or costs are significantly higher or lower than expected – will be.

A function of the information system is that it allows the business planner to model possible changes in the business – the 'What if …?' questions, as have already been discussed in Chapter 3. A range of variations on the central realistic assessment can be rapidly completed, and management must then decide what is most realistic. For most practical purposes, the impact of increasing and decreasing sales by plus 20 per cent and minus 30 per cent provides an overall view of best and worst case scenarios, although the interaction between rising costs and falling sales and other potential outcomes can be

> *For most practical purposes, the impact of increasing and decreasing sales by plus 20 per cent and minus 30 per cent provides an overall view of best and worst case scenarios.*

quickly explored if the management plan has been entered on to a computer spreadsheet.

CONTINGENCY PLANNING

Crisis or contingency management is a vital area of management skills. Even the best and most comprehensive plans can go wrong in an often bewildering number of ways. Without crisis or contingency planning to reduce the impact of problems before they occur, or deal with them effectively once they happen, SME management will always be reacting in a haphazard fashion, rather than controlling events in an ordered and structured way.

> *Without crisis or contingency planning to reduce the impact of problems before they occur, or deal with them effectively once they happen, SME management will always be reacting in a haphazard fashion, rather than controlling events in an ordered and structured way.*

To create useful contingency plans, management must first identify the problems and then determine appropriate, effective action. A step-by-step approach to the development of cost-effective contingency planning is therefore required. Here is an example of such an approach.

■ Identify the potential failure points in the plan

The first stage in crisis management is identifying the possible failure points. These are the factors that would have a serious impact on the profitability, continuing operation of the firm or physical welfare of employees or customers. In very large organisations, identifying potential combinations of these factors is extremely difficult, as the range of alternatives is very wide. For the sake of simplicity the discussion here concentrates on coping with problems one by one and not in combination.

Product quality issues

Poor product or service quality can, and does, lead to the loss of long-term profitable business. These remain common to many commercial (and non-commercial) organisations.

Customer service issues

Customers cannot be effectively served and revenue earned if there are interruptions in any of the phases between manufacture and arrival of goods or the satisfactory completion of a service. Management therefore has to consider what should be done if production, finished stock, physical distribution, product installation or servicing are either prevented from functioning or damaged in some way. In the case of a service, what to do if it fails to meet customer standards for some reason – deadlines not met, poor hygiene, rude staff and so on.

Production issues

Failures in raw material provision, components, product safety, and labour problems – the loss of trained staff, extreme behaviour of certain individuals or the cessation of work because of industrial action, say – will all significantly affect the ability of the company to meet production targets.

Information management

Loss of information about the market and customers is a potential crisis for many companies. This loss will be greatest if the company centralises all its information in some form of computer system, and least if the company has a decentralised paper system. Even this may be very vulnerable to fire and theft. Loss of information to competitors can also be a potential problem for many companies, and one that has to be controlled where the information is of substantial value, such as research and development or contract details.

▓ *Financial irregularity*

Major financial irregularities (fraud) can destroy even the largest firm. Crisis management must concentrate on reducing the potential for such irregularities to occur.

▓ *Failures in customer payment*

Another potential source of financial failure is the possibility that certain customers will not meet their commitments and attempts should be made to reduce the probability of this happening.

▓ *Changes in shareholder structure*

Substantial changes in the ownership profile of the organisation may significantly affect a company's ability to continue operating freely, as new shareholders will often have different objectives to existing ones.

▓ *Accommodation*

Damage to any or all of the buildings will also pose potentially serious problems for any organisation.

▓ *Changing sales levels, above or below plan*

Major variations from the planned level of sales will be a source of concern, and the greater the variance, the more attention it will need. These changes – positive or negative – can be important. For example, increases in sales above plan involves more working capital, increases in debtors, stocks and the like, and more staff. Decreases in sales mean problems in financing overheads, borrowings and staff pay.

▓ *Substantial increases in financing costs*

For even the largest companies, major increases in financing costs often pose severe problems and are one of the most crucial failure points.

▓ *Major changes in the macro-environment*

The planner may have made a series of erroneous assumptions about, for example, the state of the economy over the period, or failed to foresee new technology. Issues of survival may be the result as major parts of company strategy need revision.

▓ *Major changes in the competitive environment*

Our planner may have made similar errors in assumptions about the competitive environment. For example, having decided that no new competitor would appear in the market, the potential effects of such an arrival would not have been given a great deal of attention.

■ Create an effective information system

Reviewing the information system at the stage of contingency planning is useful to ensure that it is, and will continue to, provide all the data necessary to manage and control the company. An effective information system will therefore help in identifying the real source of failure among a number of possibilities. In many cases, the true cause is immediately apparent. However, where a number of contributing factors interlock – for example, declining sales caused by a mixture of product, promotional, production, distribution, pricing or personnel matters – it is important to be able to isolate where failure is occurring in order to act effectively. Management also has to decide what level constitutes failure – is a 2 per cent decline or increase in sales a substantial deviation from the plan or is it an acceptable variation?

■ Reduce the potential for failure

Having identified the likely crisis points, it is possible to reduce the potential of failure occurring. The greater the likely impact of a particular type of crisis on the company, the greater the value of the investment that should be made to prevent it. Sometimes, though, it is common sense, rather than huge investment, that is necessary. For example, where complete loss of computer records might be a substantial failure point for an organisation, investing in equipment that will automatically duplicate data in another unit or simply establishing the routine of physical transferring disks at the end of the day to some form of safekeeping, would greatly reduce the possibility of damage. Stricter quality control can also reduce the risks in this area. Small investments in employee safety can help avoid crises involving people.

■ Develop an action plan

Though appropriate investment manages problems, failure is still always a possibility and plans must bear this in mind. The detail into which these plans should go must relate to the probability of failure and the potential damage this would cause. For example, in many companies, the chances of labour disputes may be fairly high, regardless of company action taken to reduce them. If this would potentially have very harmful effects on company viability, contingency plans to deal with labour disputes should be worked out in considerable detail. Such an action plan has to consider the authority given to individual managers to take corrective action. For example, should the individual manager be responsible for dealing with complaints or safety issues within a particular part of the factory? If so, it should be made clear to the individuals concerned.

The action plan should also attempt to provide a graduated response to a particular problem, so that a series of steps can be taken as the situation becomes increasingly serious. Thus, when sales fall by 3 per cent it may be appropriate to review sales promotional and sales force policy. When they fall by 5 per cent, stock levels and promotional investment need to be reviewed. When they fall by 10 per cent another set of plans come into effect, and so on.

■ Communicate

A key management task is to ensure that all relevant personnel are informed of all the main features of the contingency plan, including what actions to take to reduce potential failure and what should be done when problems arise. Specific training improves management's ability to act quickly and effectively – most appropriate in such cases as fires where physical safety issues are involved.

Once these plans have been created, they need to be reviewed from time to time to take account of new circumstances. On a practical basis, reviews of the business plan should include a consideration of the contingency issues, to ensure that new information and new demands on the organisation are properly accounted for.

ACTION PLANNING

The final control element should be the creation of an action plan, on a month-by-month basis, to include the action or task that needs to be completed, how its achievement will be measured and the individual responsible for its completion. An example of how this can be developed is shown in Table 8.2, for the month of January, with the tasks, the milestones or measures of achievement and the individuals who are to carry it out.

For new product or service development, the action planning needs to be much more detailed. The project is divided into a whole series of tasks, each with associated timescales, measurements of task achievement (milestones) and resource requirements. This enables the project planner to identify those items that are on the 'critical path' – that is, those that must be completed on time and to budget to ensure that the overall project is also completed on time and to budget, and which must be closely monitored and controlled.

Table 8.2 A monthly action plan

Month	Sales and marketing	New product development	Production	Personnel	Finance
Jan	Completion of Megastore promo *Delivered leaflets* **G. Donnelly**	Presentation of A1 *Presentation* **A. Bernard**	Mainman unit fully operational *95% efficiency for five days* **K. Roux**	WP training complete *Certification of 95% participants* **M. Flower**	Grant availability *Presentation* **C. Planter**
Feb					
March					
April					
May					
June					
July					
Aug					
Sept					
Oct					
Nov					
Dec					

SUMMARY

As a series of checks on the business plan, completing the assessment of assumptions, including a consideration of the level of risk, running a sensitivity analysis and drawing up a detailed action plan will all ensure that the plan that has been produced is indeed SURE:

- **Soundly based;**
- **Understands the issues;**
- **Realistic;**
- **Experienced personnel handle the major issues.**

The business health check

INTRODUCTION

From the viewpoint of an external adviser to SMEs, it is valuable to assess the health of the business by identifying its major strengths and weaknesses prior to a detailed analysis of the management information system.

Over the years, I have developed a business health check to quickly sum up the business in a rough and ready way. A healthy business has a high score, while a business with a low score needs help and assistance. The scoring system attempts to produce an overall index that can be used to compare company with company, and is of value to business angels and corporate investors in identifying strengths and weaknesses in the commercial environment of the company – elements that financial analyses inadequately reveal. Here, the case study companies are compared (see Table 9.1).

Table 9.1 A comparative business health check of Brainstorm and Softawater

Factor	Brainstorm	Softawater
Market growth		
Profitability growth		
Product/service quality rating		
Product/service innovation		
Market share		
Seasonality of sales		
Stability of customer base		
Information availability		
Average equipment age		
Skills		
Administration versus line management		
Previous history		
Debt equity		

The health check is based on 15 issues. These are outlined below, but you will find that you have already encountered many of them in the business plan analysis.

MARKET GROWTH

Market growth is measured here as the percentage change over three years. A business in a declining market is one that faces potentially serious problems. Where a business is operating across a range of markets, with some declining and expanding, the proportion of turnover in each sector, multiplied by the growth or decline will provide the final figure.

Example

Market growth of 50 per cent over 3 years, scores 50. Market decline of 10 per cent over 3 years, scores −10.

PROFITABILITY GROWTH

Those businesses with an improving profitability record face a potentially less problematic future than those with declining profitability. The useful ratio here is the gross profit margin rather than the net margin.

Profit margin growth over last 3 years = percentage change x 10

Examples

Profit margin for year 1 is 15 per cent, profit margin for year 3 is 20 per cent, so improvement = 5 per cent x 10 = 50.

Profit margin for year 1 is 20 per cent, for year 3 it is 15 per cent = −5 x 10 = −50.

PRODUCT OR SERVICE QUALITY RATING

Those businesses that are perceived to have the highest quality of service or products in a particular industry are those with the greatest potential. Here the SME must compare itself with the leader in its industry. How close does your company come to achieving the highest quality products or services – entirely (100 per cent, score 100), close (80–90 per cent, score 50), a distance from it (50–80 per cent, score 30), far, far away (30–50 – score 10)? Inevitably, such an assessment is a subjective one.

> *Those businesses that are perceived to have the highest quality of service or products in a particular industry are those with the greatest potential.*

PRODUCT OR SERVICE INNOVATION RATING

Similarly, how does the company compare with the leaders in the industry in the way it develops new products or services (see Chapters 2 and 5, Table 5.11)? Where there is information on the product development of the industry leaders, with published data on the percentage of turnover coming from products introduced within the last year, two years and so on, it may be possible to quantify the comparison. Otherwise, again, it is subjective. How close does your company come to achieving the highest level of industry product development – entirely (100 per cent, score 100), close (80–90 per cent, score 50), a distance from it (50–80 per cent, score 30), far, far away (30–50 per cent, score 10)?

MARKET SHARE

Companies with good market shares will be inherently stronger than those without. The value of the market share is always relative to the market in which the firm operates. Is it local, regional or national? What is the size of the competitors? The most sensible calculation is to measure the current market share of the company, divide this by the market share of the top three competitors and multiply this figure by 100.

Example

Market share is 10 per cent, top 3 competitors' 20 per cent = 50 per cent, score 50.

SEASONALITY OF SALES

A company with a highly seasonal business is one that is less stable than one with a flat pattern of sales. The easiest way to calculate this is to compare the sales level in the quietest month with that of the busiest month and multiply by 100.

Example

Sales in the slowest month (3) = 200, in busiest month (4) = 260, 200/260 = 0.8 x 100 = score of 80;

Sales in the slowest month (3) = 50, in the busiest month (4) = 500 = 50/500 = 0.1 x 100 = score of 10.

STABILITY OF THE CUSTOMER BASE

A company with a continually changing customer base will have higher costs and the generation of cash flow is less assured. A good score also provides a meaure of how responsive the company is to its customers and how effectively it services them.

Obviously any analysis of this type needs to take account of takeovers and closures and remove them from the customer list. The calculation is then based on those customers that were serviced by the company three years ago, compared with the position today, multiplied by 100.

Example

60 customers remain today from the original 100 customers of 3 years ago = 60/100 = 0.6 × 100 = score of 60

5 customers remain today from the 100 of 3 years ago = 5/100 = 0.05 × 100 = score of 5.

INFORMATION AVAILABILITY

Companies that are well provided for in terms of information are likely to understand their business best. Scoring the availability of information in the major areas of the business will provide a good measure of how effectively the business is being managed. Some items of information are more crucial than others, so the complete availability of the information in a particular area needs to be ranked accordingly (see Chapter 3). Complete availability of information is scored as shown in Table 9.2.

> **Companies that are well provided for in terms of information are likely to understand their business best.**

Table 9.2 Scoring the availability of key information

Items	Score
Cash flow	20
Profit and loss	20
Balance sheet	10
Financial ratios	10
Personnel ratios	10
Production	20
Marketing	10

AVERAGE AGE OF EQUIPMENT

For both manufacturing and service companies, the age of equipment is a vital factor in improving the quality and speed of production. The average age of the equipment in years will determine the position of the company:

0–3 years, score 100;
3–6 years, score 50;
6–10 years, score 25;
10+ years, score 0.

SKILLS

The better the skills level, the greater is the likelihood of the company developing new products, effectively servicing customers and running the business profitably and efficiently. As shown in Table 9.3, there are three categories of staff that need to be considered:

- line;
- administration;
- senior management;

and five categories of activity:

- production or service supply;
- finance;
- sales;
- marketing;
- information technology (IT).

The better the skills level, the greater is the likelihood of the company developing new products, effectively servicing customers and running the business profitably and efficiently.

Measuring the average skills level in each part of the business using a 1–5 (novice to expert) ranking, businesses will vary from a basic skills level of 15 per cent to a high skills level of 75 per cent (see Chapter 2, page 25).

Table 9.3   Table to use to record skills level scores

Line	Administration	Senior management
Production		
Finance		
Sales		
Marketing		
IT		

ADMINISTRATION VERSUS LINE MANAGEMENT

High levels of administrative staff relative to the total number employed in the company will often have a significant impact on the performance of that company. Excessive layers of administrative staff slow decision making, create difficulties in customer contact, and raise costs and breakeven points.

Excessive layers of administrative staff slow decision making, create difficulties in customer contact, and raise costs and breakeven points.

Numbers of line staff/numbers of admin staff × 10.

217

Example

If there are 50 line staff and 10 administrative staff = 50/10 = 5 × 10 = 50.

PREVIOUS HISTORY OF KEY STAFF

Previous successes tend to breed current success, while previous failures are suggestive of future failures. The more failures, the greater the problems the company is likely to face.

The scoring system used here is based on the absolute number of business failures each individual has been involved in, and does not involve any calculation. Scoring is as follows:

1–2 failures among key staff, score 100;

3–5 failures, score 50;

6–10 failures, score 10.

TRENDS IN FIXED COSTS

How fixed costs have moved against sales in the recent past is an important measure of the health of the company (see Chapter 2). As sales increase, fixed costs should decline as a proportion of total costs. The speed of this decline provides an indication of how effectively the company is managing growth or, if sales are declining, how the company is managing to control its cost base.

(Sales in year 3/fixed costs in year 3)/(Sales in year 1/fixed costs in year 1) × 100.

Example

(Sales in year 3 = 1,500/fixed costs of 210)/
(Sales in year 1 = 1,000/fixed costs of 200) × 100
= (1,500/210)/(1,000/200) × 100
= 1.42 × 100
= 142.

DEBT TO EQUITY LEVELS

The calculation of debt to equity levels provides a measure of how well capitalised the company is and how influenced it may be by major changes in the level of sales and/or interest rate movements (see Chapter 3). In order to convert the gearing ratio to a common basis with the other figures – that is 100 is healthy, 10 is poor – it is necessary to invert the gearing ratio:

1/level of debt $\times$ 10.

Example
If the debt percentage is 60, the score is 16.6: 1/0.6 x 10.

INTEREST COVER

Well-covered interest payments are a sign that the business will face few problems paying its way, even if it suffers a downturn in sales or profitability (see Chapter 3).

The scoring system in this case is based on the number of times the pre-interest earnings cover the interest payments. Thus, the interest cover figures and score are:

1–1.5 times, score 10;
1.51–2, score 30;
2.01–3, score 50;
3.01+, score 100.

SUMMARY

The value of the business health check is that it provides outside observers of the business with a rapid checklist that should enable them to identify particular problem areas that require additional attention.

For the SME planner, it provides an indication as to how outside observers are likely to assess their business, and provides an early warning about those issues that need action.

Index